What Now Lord?

Now that I am a Christ Follower.

David S. Massey

Copyright © 2003 by David S. Massey

What Now Lord?
by David S. Massey

Printed in the United States of America

ISBN 1-594672-22-9

All rights reserved. No part of this publication may be reproduced or transmitted in any form or by any means without written permission of the author.

Bible Quotations are taken from the following versions of the Bible:

KJV
Scripture quotations marked KJV are taken from the Holy Bible, King James Version. The text of the King James Version is in the Public Domain.
RSV
Scripture quotations marked RSV are taken from the Holy Bible, Revised Standard Version, © 1946, 1952, 1971 by the Division of Christian Education of the National Council of Churches in the United States of America.
The Revised Standard Version, (New York: O) © 1973, 1977.
NEB
Scripture quotations marked NEB are taken from The New English Bible, © 1961, 1970 by The Delegates of the O and The Syndics of the C.
NRSV
Scripture quotations marked NRSV are taken from the Holy Bible, New Revised Standard Version, © 1989 by the Division of Christian Education of the National Council of Churches in the United States of America.
The New Revised Standard Version, (Nashville, Tennessee: Thomas Nelson Publishers, Inc.) © 1989.

NKJV
The Holy Bible, New King James Version, (Nashville, Tennessee: Thomas Nelson Publishers, Inc.) © 1982.

NAS/NASB
Scripture quotations marked NASB or NAS are taken from the New American Standard Bible, © 1960, 1962, 1963, 1968, 1971, 1972, 1973, 1975, 1977, 1995 by The Lockman Foundation. Used by permission.
The New American Standard Bible, (La Habra, California: T) © 1977.

NIV
Scripture quotations marked NIV are from the Holy Bible, New International Version, © 1973, 1978, 1984 International Bible Society. Used by permission of Zondervan Bible Publishers.
The New International Version, (Grand Rapids, MI: Z) © 1984.

TEV
Scripture quotations marked TEV are taken from The Good News Bible, The Bible in Today's English Version. New Testament © 1966, 1971, 1976 by the A.

TLB
Scripture quotations marked TLB are taken from The Living Bible, © 1971 owned by assignment by KNT Charitable Trust. All rights reserved.
The Living Bible, (Wheaton, Ill.: T) © 1997.

NLT
Holy Bible, New Living Translation, (Wheaton, IL: T) © 1996.

NCV
The New Century Version, (Dallas, Texas: Word Publishing) © 1987, 1988, 1991.

TM
The Message, Eugene Peterson (Pinion Press; 2nd edition © March 2003)

Xulon Press
www.XulonPress.com

Xulon Press books are available in bookstores everywhere, and on the Web at www.XulonPress.com.

Dedications:

To my wife, Grayson:
My personal Holy Spirit on earth,
you bring out the best in me and put up with my worst.

To our kids Morgan, Mary and Bobby who put up with and
understood Dad hiding behind his laptop on countless nights,
thanks for loving me unconditionally.

To Mom and Dad:
Thanks for loving and encouraging me all these years.

To my Wednesday night small group:
I love you all.

To my friend and editor, Jan Moser:
Thanks for your tireless efforts to make sense
out of my spelling and grammar.

To Our Lord:
Thanks for putting up with my antics with your love,
grace and mercy. Apart from You I am nothing.

Contents

Introduction ix

Chapter One – The Gospel 13

Chapter Two – Hearing God's Callings 21
    Part 1 – Reconizing God's Call 21
    Part 2 – The First Person 23
    Part 3 – Clear Direction 24
    Part 4 – Authoritative Commands 26
    Part 5 – Great Promise 27
    Part 6 – Change 28

Chapter Three – Drifting Away 31

Chapter Four – The Prodigal Son 35
    Part 1 – Give Me 35
    Part 2 – I Want it Now! 37
    Part 3 – The Bottom 38
    Part 4 – Reflection 40
    Part 5 – Restoration 42
    Part 6 – Homecoming 44

Chapter Five – Spiritual Disciplines 47
    Part 1 – Introduction 47
    Part 2 – Bible Reading 48
    Part 3 – Prayer 51
    Part 4 – Use A Spiritual Journal 53

Part 5 – Fasting 55
Part 6 – Solitude and Silence..56

Chapter Six – Balancing the Gauges 59
Part 1 – Running Fast!..59
Part 2 – Devote Daily 61
Part 3 – Worship Weekly 63
Part 4 – Measure Monthly 65

Chapter Seven – Small Groups And Accountability ...69
Part 1 – Four Relationships We All Need.........................69
Part 2 – Teaching and Sharing..71
Part 3 – Accountability..72
Part 4 – Choosing a Partner 73
Part 5 – Being Held Accountable 74

Chapter Eight – Twelve Steps for Christian Living 77
Part 1 – Powerless...77
Part 2 – Belief...79
Part 3 – Decision Time 81
Part 4 – Inventory Time 83
Part 5 – Confession Time 85
Part 6 – Contemplation...87
Part 7 – Removal 88
Part 8 – Making Amends..91
Part 9 – Make Amends 92
Part 10 – Continuation..95
Part 11 – Prayer 96
Part 12 – An Awakening...99

Chapter Nine – Going Out 103
Part 1 – Personal Evangelism..103
Part 2 – Evangelism Approaches.....................................105
Part 3 – Caveats of Evangelism.......................................108

Introduction

In his book, The Man In The Mirror, Pat Morley writes, "Cultural Christianity means to pursue the God we want instead of the God who is. It is the tendency to be shallow in our understanding of God, wanting Him to be more of a gentle, grandfather type who spoils us and lets us have our own way. It is sensing a need for God, but on our own terms. It wants the God we have underlined in our Bibles without wanting the rest of Him, too. It is God relative instead of God absolute." The first time I read that paragraph it grabbed my heart; it twisted, tossed, and turned me; and it left a permanent imprint on my life.

I realized then, that I was a cultural Christian and not a biblical Christian. What happened along the way? What happened between the time I accepted Jesus Christ as my Savior as a young child growing up in the church, and now. What happened during my pilgrimage? I fear what happened to me, happens to many Christians today.

As long as I can remember, I've considered myself a Christian. I mean, I'm an American—and isn't this God's country? Aren't we a Christian nation? Aren't all Americans Christians? My Mama and Daddy dedicated me as a baby to the church. Every Sunday our family went to church, Sunday school, and Sunday night devotion and prayer time. One Sunday, at the age of 12, I was baptized. We said the blessing at every meal. My mama read Psalm 23 to me every night before bed, and I always said my prayers before going to sleep. I even read Christian magazines for kids. My mom and dad did a great job in rearing up their children to be Christians.

I had it all, so I thought—I was an American, had a Christian family, and grew up attending church. So I thought I had it all. But something—someone was missing from the picture. That someone was Jesus.

What happened along the way? Why was Christ missing from my life? I look back now and realize He was missing because I didn't want Him in my life. I just wanted a God of convenience. A God who is there when I need Him, how I need Him, and for any reason that suited me at the time I needed Him. Voltaire once said, "God created man in His own image; man has been returning the favor every since." Well, I had created the perfect God. In college He was a God I placed on the bookshelf, taking Him down only when I was struggling and needed Him for a little while. Then it was back to the bookshelf. Like a fire extinguisher God, He was there just in case of an emergency. Now I look back on how I treated Him and realize what a patient God He is!

After college I married my college sweetheart. Then it was off to the family business in order to get, not earn, my slice of the American dream. My wife and I started attending church. It made sense. All our friends were going there as well as many of the people I did business with. I thought, This is great, I can go to church on Sunday in order to produce some business for Monday. Learn some Christianity on Sunday, put God in my desk drawer on Monday, and take Him back the next Sunday. This was Christianity at its best.

But one day, I guess God got tired of being in that desk drawer—He had other plans for my life. My wife and I started going to a Sunday school class that was different from our other experiences. It wasn't the Sunday morning "Rotary Club" class. I didn't do business with the people in the class. The class was studying the real meaning of Christmas. The Holy Spirit ambushed me for the first time in a long time. The simplicity of realizing who Christ is struck my heart. (By the way, that was the best Christmas I ever experienced.) And that was just the beginning. My heart stirred more and more and I wanted to know this Person, this Savior, Jesus Christ. The Holy Spirit had changed my heart, and instead of putting God back in my desk drawer on Monday morning, I let Him stay out a little longer.

What Now Lord?

My new interest in Christ soon sputtered. I became disillusioned with church once again. God went back in the drawer when He wasn't convenient to me—or when He got in the way. But for some reason I became increasingly disturbed with going to church with cultural Christians who were my best friends on Sunday, only to stab me in the back on Monday during business. The picture just didn't look right.

There's a trend in the Church today. This trend may be an old trend, but it's one I've experienced and recognize even today. This trend is to preach the "gospel of addition". The gospel of addition is simply adding Jesus Christ to your present life, without subtracting your sinful ways in your life. Paul said in Acts 26:20, "I preached that they should repent and turn to God and prove their repentance by their deeds." Paul is saying that we should add Jesus, subtract (repent) our sins, and prove this by our actions. What we say we believe and what we do must be consistent. We're not only challenged to become a believer, but a doer of the Word as well. The picture in our hearts must equal the picture we paint by our deeds. Think about it. Are your actions consistent with your values? Are they consistent with the way God wants them to be, not just with what you want?

Aha, another ambush by the Holy Spirit. My actions need to reflect my beliefs, thus allowing the image of God to be seen in me. I need to stop reinventing God and allow Him to mold me.

James said it well in James 1:22-25, *"Do not merely listen to the Word, and so deceive yourselves. Do what it says. Anyone who listens to the Word but does not do what it says is like a man, who looks at his face in a mirror and, after looking at himself, goes away and immediately forgets what he looks like. But the man who looks intently into the perfect law that gives freedom, and continues to do this, not forgetting what he has heard, but doing it-he will be blessed in what he does." (NIV)*

Whoa, the Holy Spirit does it again, another ambush! Do not only listen and read the Word, but be a doer of the Word as well. What's another way to say it? Don't just talk the talk or walk the walk, but walk the talk. Fully surrender your life to Him.

I'm continually amazed at the patience God has with me. When the timing is perfect, He nudges me along the path of growth in Him. One such nudge happened when He directed my wife and me to another church. A place where many of the people are doers of the Word and the teaching is biblical and challenging. A place where the real God is honored and the God of convenience is put to rest. Now, in our walk with the Lord it's all coming together—we strive to live fully surrendered lives to Christ. Now God stays out of the desk drawer. He's on top, in full view for all to see! Yes the journey is long, if fact, it's never-ending. The journey seems slow to us, and it's often bumpy, but it's worth taking. It's worth being patient, worth the sacrifices, and worth subtracting the sins. Why is it worth it? It's worth it because of the addition of Jesus to our lives. Take the journey, give yourself fully to Him, and worship the God who is, not the God you've invented for your convenience. It's worth the greatest value system known to humanity. It will grab your heart, core out the hard parts, and give you a better way of living on earth with your heavenly Father. What now Lord?

Chapter One

The Gospel

1 Corinthians 15:1 "Now, the faithful, I want to remind you of the gospel I preached to you, which you received and on which you have taken your stand." (NIV)

Ah, the gospel. We throw that word around a lot. We say with enthusiasm, "My pastor is preaching the gospel!" Or sometimes we say, "Man, what you need is the gospel."

Just what is the gospel? I can remember asking my mother that question when I was 11 or 12 years old. Her answer to me was "Son, the gospel is the good news about Jesus Christ being our Savior." As always, mom was right. But exactly what is the gospel?

It's pretty simple. The gospel was only about 25-years-old when Paul wrote to the people of Corinth in his letter. They seemingly had complicated it in just a short time. We've had nearly 2000-years to complicate God's plan for us. Paul clearly lays it out for us in the next passage.

1 Corinthians 15:3-5 "For what I received I passed on to you as of first importance: that Christ died for our sins according to the Scriptures, that he was buried, that he was raised on the third day according to the Scriptures, and that he appeared to Peter, and then to the twelve. (NIV)

In other words, the gospel is simply this:
Jesus died for our sins. (He didn't just die; he died for us, in place of us.)
Jesus was buried.
Jesus was raised on the third day.
He appeared to several people after he came back to life.

That's it folks. Add anything to this, and you don't have the gospel of Jesus Christ, take away anything and you have no gospel. In fact, many cults sound Christian, but when you look deeper into them, they all deny part of the gospel and some even add to the list.

What do you and I do to this list? What do we do that isn't the gospel? The gospel isn't doing, doing, and doing some more to please God or earn His grace. The gospel isn't attending a worship service every Sunday (although I recommend it, for other reasons). The gospel isn't about us doing something. Nor is the gospel about being a religious person. Jesus Christ did it all for us. He alone is faithful for us. It is His faithfulness that makes us right with God—not ours.

Too often we spell religion or the gospel with two letters, "d-o". You need to do this or do that. Often we feel like we need to be doing, doing, and then doing some more. Folks, religion isn't spelled d-o. It is spelled "d-o-n-e". It's what Jesus Christ has done for us. It is His faithfulness to go to the cross—in our place—that saves us from a Christ-less eternity.

I'm not saying, "Look folks, just accept Christ and don't do anything." To the contrary, my passion during this life is "growing people up in Christ." Nothing energizes me more than to watch a person grow in their faith and become a little more like Christ each week—myself included. What I am saying is this, let's stop complicating the gospel and simply start living day-to-day in appreciation and gratitude for what Christ has done for us. Let's start living moment-by-moment full of His love, His grace, and His mercy. Let's start showing the fruit of the Spirit to those around us. Let's use the little piece of earth where God has placed us for His glory and honor. It's simple if you think about it. Let's take a deeper look into each part of the gospel.

I have often had non-believers and even Christian friends ask me, "Just why did Jesus have to die?" It's a great question and one that we as Christians need to be able to answer. Jesus died in place of us. It's you and I that should be on the cross. Let's look at four reasons why He died for us.

1. He died as our substitute.

Romans 3:25-26 "For God sent Christ Jesus to take the punishment for our sins and to end all God's anger against us. He used Christ's blood and our faith as the means of saving us from his wrath. In this way he was being fair, even though he did not punish those who sinned in former times. For he was looking forward to the time when Christ would come and take away those sins. And now in these days also he can receive sinners in this same way because Jesus took away their sins. But isn't this unfair for God to let criminals go free, and say that they are innocent? No, for he does it by their trust in Jesus who took away their sins." (LB)

2. He died to be our Advocate to reconcile us to God or simply said, to make us right with God.

2 Corinthians 5:21 "For God took the sinless Christ and poured into him our sins. Then, in exchange, he poured God's goodness into us!" (LB)

1 John 2:1-2 My dear children, I am writing this to you so that you will not sin. But if you do sin, there is someone to plead for you before the Father. He is Jesus Christ, the one who pleases God completely. (NLT)

3. He died to be our Mediator and to make us partners in the New Covenant.

Luke 22:20 "After supper he gave them another glass of wine, saying, "This wine is the token of God's new agreement to save you—an agreement sealed with the blood I shall pour out to purchase back your souls." (LB)

    4. He died to grant us everlasting life and defeat our number one enemy, death.

John 3:16 "For God loved the world so much that he gave his only Son so that anyone who believes in him shall not perish but have eternal life." (NIV)

Jesus didn't just disappear; He was buried. It's interesting that only Paul mentions the burial.

1 Corinthians 15:4 "...that he was buried, that he was raised on the third day according to the Scriptures." (NIV)

Why is the burial important? It shows us that Christ died on the cross. He did not just pass out, and He did not just go away somewhere to hide, only to reappear. Throughout the Bible it's awesome how God always prevails and how those against God's plan unknowingly work for the plan. The Jewish and Roman leaders made certain that Jesus was indeed dead and buried. They made certain that all the witnesses knew without a doubt that Christ had died. Then, when the tomb was found empty, they unknowingly verified the truth of the resurrection, by taking such extreme measures to make sure no one could enter the tomb and steal the body. For someone to resurrect, they must first die. Likewise, something in us must die as well when we become Christians. Paul identifies our baptism with Christ's burial in the following verse:

Romans 6:4 "We were therefore buried with him through baptism into death in order that, just as Christ was raised from the dead through the glory of the Father, we too may live a new life." (NIV)

As a Christian, are you living a new life or clinging to the old one? It is the hardest struggle we face every moment of every day.

Nowhere in the Bible does it say, "Once you become a Christian, living the Christian life is instantly easy." It's a lifetime journey. For me, it's burying the old life a little bit at a time—a slow and sometimes frustrating process. Here are three facts to remember that help me. I pray they help you in your journey to be more like Christ.

As newness comes, there will always be tension with the old life. In all change there is tension for us, whether it's a policy change at work, a scheduling change at school, or a change in our home environment. Paul said it best:

Romans 7:15 "I do not understand what I do. For what I want to do I do not do, but what I hate I do." (NIV)

We must build a climate of love in all that we do, a love-for-God and a love-for-people attitude. By affirming one another with the love of Christ we will grow in Christ. When we start treating others and seeing others through Christ's eyes, we can't help but become more like Christ.

Ephesians 5:2 "Live a life of love just as Christ loved us and gave himself for us as a sweet-smelling offering and sacrifice to God." (NCV)

We must cling to our faith so we will reach Christ-likeness when we are resurrected. Without Christ, death is our number one enemy; it's the enemy that we cannot overcome with force, power, science, or governments. It can only be overcome through our Savior, Jesus.

Philippians 1:6 "Being confident of this very thing, that He who has begun a good work in you will complete it until the day of Jesus Christ." (NKJV)

And the day of Jesus Christ will come, my friends. We will change from being "copies" of Adam and dead to sin, to being copies of Christ and alive for eternity with Him. What an awesome hope and promise.

Let's look at a few aspects of the gospel and how they apply to us.

1 Corinthians 15:4-6 "That he was buried and was raised to life on the third day as the Scriptures say; and that he was seen by Peter and then by the twelve apostles. After that, Jesus was seen by more than five hundred of the believers at the same time. Most of them are still living today, but some have died." (NCV)

No other religion claims that their leader was resurrected from the dead. Christianity is based solely on the life, death, and resurrection of Jesus Christ. Thank God it isn't based on any of us! Notice in this passage that Paul states that many of the witnesses were still living at the time this letter was written. Think about it a moment. If I wrote today that after much study and research I have found that the world is flat. My e-mail box would be overflowing. Letters would tell me at best that I am mistaken, and at worst that I am a liar and a fraud. Likewise, if the resurrection weren't true, at least one of the five hundred witnesses would have spoken up and said, "Whoa, this Paul guy is a liar and a fraud." The resurrection is the final convincing evidence that Jesus is who He claims to be, the Messiah.

So, you ask, what does this mean to me? Glad you asked! It means that we, too, can conquer our number one enemy, death. Without Christ as our Savior we have two deaths, one physical and one spiritual. With Christ we have two births—one physical and one spiritual—and the victory is that we only experience physical death. Our spiritual life will continue forever.

You know what I think Heaven will be like? Do you know that wonderful feeling you have when you feel God's presence? It's that feeling of overwhelming love God has for you. It's that feeling of indescribable gratitude for Him. I get that feeling when I am closest to God, close to His will for my life. My whole body relaxes and I feel one with God. That's the feeling I think heaven is going to be like, a feeling of oneness with God. And in Heaven, the feeling never goes away.

1 John 3:2 "Dear friends, now we are children of God, and we have not yet been shown what we will be in the future. But we know that when Christ comes again, we will be like him, because we will see him as he really is." (NCV)

We will go from being carbon copies of Adam, to being carbon copies of Christ. So what does that mean? We will go from struggling with sin every day, to being free from sin. We will go from having physical and mental ailments to complete wholeness. We will be transformed into perfect beings, living with our Holy God for all eternity.

It is our destiny to be like Christ. We struggle everyday to become just a little more like Him while we are here on earth. We will never fully succeed here on earth, but we will in Heaven. Christ's resurrection and ours are intermingled; to deny one or the other is to deny the gospel. When we accept Christ, we have an inner-transformation. Change occurs; our heart, our priorities, our values, our purposes, and our meaning for life change. God constantly refines our inner beings. When we're resurrected we will be made complete. Our perfect spiritual bodies will replace our physical bodies. Then we will be complete, new on the inside and new on the outside. That is our promise as Christ-followers. John sums it all up well in Revelation:

Revelation 21:4 "He will wipe away every tear from their eyes, and there will be no more death, sadness, crying, or pain, because all the old ways are gone." (NCV)

When you see a cross, picture yourself on the cross, with someone about to hammer the spikes into your hands and feet. At the last minute, as the hammer is about to slam a piercing nail into your hands, a voice yells from the crowd, "Stop!" You're startled. The man with the hammer stops, the crowd around you looks toward the one calling for a halt as he approaches the cross. The man tells the guard, "Release this person on that cross; I will go in his place." Of course that man is Jesus Christ, who did exactly that for us. He took our place on the cross for our sins, so that one day we could be like

Him and live with Him in heaven. What an awesome God!

Now I believe I understand the good news of the gospel, but now what Lord?

Chapter Two

Hearing God's Calls

Part 1 – Recognizing God's Call

One of the most frequently asked questions I hear when teaching Bible studies is, "How can I know God's calling for my life?" I'm sure you have often asked the same question. Follow me through the following steps to test the decisions you face in life against some relevant, biblical principles that I have learned and relearned over the years. Walk with me as I lay out these principles to help us judge between our will and God's call.

Often when we think about God's calling, we think of professional ministers. We harbor this misconception that God only calls people into full-time ministry. The other common mistake we make is waiting for that lightning-bolt experience that will show us God's calling for our lives as clearly as a new, crisply unfolded road map. More often than not, God only gives us a small piece of the map at a time. For example, look at God's calling to Abraham in Genesis.

Genesis 12:1 "Then the LORD told Abram, "Leave your country, your relatives, and your father's house, and go to the land that I will show you." (NLT)

Notice the call is to "leave your country," and the yet-to-be-seen calling is to "the land I will show you." God does not say to Abraham, "Leave your country and come to Canaan, where I will make you the father of a great nation." God simply says, "Leave, then I will show you." My paraphrase of this verse is, "Abraham, first trust Me, then I will show you where your calling is leading you."

I believe God uses many different callings throughout our lives to guide us along our journeys. I agree there is usually an overall big-picture calling for people, but God still uses promptings and other callings along the way to help us. In other words, the big-picture calling may be for you to be a schoolteacher, a sales person, or a stay-at-home parent. Callings guide you along the way to fully develop you into the schoolteacher, sales person, or stay-at-home person God has planned for you to be. When did God begin dealing with you? He started before the beginning of time. Look at the following verse:

Ephesians 1:4-5 "Long ago, even before he made the world, God loved us and chose us in Christ to be holy and without fault in his eyes. His unchanging plan has always been to adopt us into his own family by bringing us to himself through Jesus Christ. And this gave him great pleasure." (NLT)

None of the biblical principles and truths that I am going to lay out over the next few pages will work unless you have answered God's foundational calling. His first and main calling is for you to accept Jesus Christ as your Savior and Lord. I can say without a doubt or hesitation this is the main calling God has for your life.

1 Corinthians 1:9 "God, who has called you into fellowship with his Son Jesus Christ our Lord, is faithful." (NLT)

John 3:16 "For God so loved the world that He gave His only begotten Son, that whoever believes in Him should not perish but have everlasting life." (NKJ)

The five characteristics of God's callings are:

In the first person
Have clear direction
Authoritative commands
Great promise
Create change

In part two we will begin to look at the first of five characteristics of God's callings, "In the first person." My prayer is for this series to help you stop, think, and listen for God's callings in your life. I look forward to our journey together.

Part 2 – The First Person

Suddenly during the sermon, the church felt empty of everyone except for the pastor and me. The lights seemed dim and low. It was as if God was speaking one-on-one with me through the pastor.

Driving down the road listening to a preacher on the radio, something clicked within me. I was crying and felt overwhelmed as I realized that God was speaking to me through someone on the radio. I knew at that moment, that I had to pull over and listen.

In another instance, as I was reading the Bible, my eyes raced faster and faster across the words, because what I was reading was speaking directly to me about a current crisis in my own life. I read it again, thinking to myself, "Yes Lord, that is what I've been going through, and yes Lord, I know You can handle this; Your Word tells me so."

Ever have experiences like these? They are callings to us, directly from God. These are always one-on-one, person-to-person, direct-from-God callings. This is the first of five characteristics of God's callings.

When people say to me, "I think I've been called into foreign missions," the first question out of my mouth is, "Tell me about the calling." They may respond, "Well, so-and-so said they were thinking about me and thought I would be good in foreign missions—why, they even tracked me down in the parking lot at church to tell me!" If they say that, of course the next question I ask is, "But what did God say to you when He called you?" Their usual response is "Huh?"

See the difference? The first three examples are in the first person; they are one-to-one, direct callings from God. The foreign mission example is in the second person. This is not a good quality calling, although I admit it may be the beginning of a call.

Genesis 17:3 "Abram fell face down, and God said to him, "As for me, this is my covenant with you: You will be the father of many nations. No longer will you be called Abram; your name will be Abraham, for I have made you a father of many nations." (NLT)

Throughout the Bible, we read about God speaking directly to people, or speaking through "an angel of the Lord." Can God do this today? Certainly! I believe today God has chosen to speak to us in the first person in three ways. First, God speaks through His Word, the Bible. Secondly, God speaks through His people—in other words, through fellow Christians. Thirdly, God speaks through an inner prompting of the Holy Spirit, who lives in everyone who has accepted Christ as his or her Savior.

Okay, great—the first characteristic of God's calling is that it is person-to-person. "So David," you ask, "what's the application of this principle?" Glad you asked.

You will never hear God's calling unless you are where God calls.

If you read the Bible regularly, God can use the Bible to speak to you. If you go to church, a Bible study, or seek counsel from other Christians, then you will hear God speaking to you through others. If you pray, slow down, stop, and listen to the inner prompting of the Holy Spirit who lives in you, then you will hear God's callings. But if you continue to fill your life with busyness, noise, static, and avoidance of God's methods of speaking, then you cannot hear the person-to-person callings.

Part 3 – Clear Direction

As a real estate appraiser, I'm often asked, "What is the hardest part of your job?" With tongue-in-cheek, but speaking from experience, I'll respond, "Finding the house."

I am well prepared to find houses. In fact, there are so many maps in my car, that it has become a fire hazard! Even with all my maps, sometimes I still cannot find the house without calling the owner from my car and saying, "I'm here. How do I get to where you are?" Most of the time, the problem is that there's no address on the house, driveway, or mailbox.

True callings from God give us clear directions to follow. God is not going to call us toward what He wants for us, only to leave the "number off the mailbox." The frustration for us comes when God decides to dole out only a portion of the directions. God will say, "You are here; I want you there. When you get there, I will tell you where to go next." Notice how God calls Moses to bring His people out of Egypt.

Exodus 3:10 "So now I am sending you to the king of Egypt. Go! Bring my people, the Israelites, out of Egypt!" (NCV)

Our problem is that like Moses, we want all the directions and details at once. If the complete set of directions is not laid out before us, sometimes we give up hope and lose faith in God. We wonder why God abandoned us, when in fact we have abandoned Him. I would never find some of the houses to appraise if I did not simply call the owners for more directions. When we are feeling lost along the way in our lives, we have a direct line to God through prayer. Don't forget that God always wants what is best for us. He always wants us to ask Him for directions. I used to fear arriving in Heaven and hearing God saying, "David, I was waiting to give you the last part of the directions, but you never asked."

So, how do we apply this to our lives? How do we know if our direction is from God—and not from our own wants? Test the call. Get your feet wet. I've had people tell me, "I think God is calling me out of the secular marketplace and into a job with a Christian organization."

I will always respond by saying, "Great, test the waters by doing a little volunteer work in the field. Send out some résumés and seek counsel from others that work in that arena."

If you are moving in the direction that God has called you, He will continue to move you in that direction. Where God guides, God will provide.

Do you have a call to make today?

Part 4 – Authoritative Commands

Genesis 35:1 "God said to Jacob, "Go to the city of Bethel and live there." (NCV)

My three kids are 17, 15 and 10. The oldest two are girls and the youngest is a boy. There is one lesson that I am continuing to learn as a parent, especially with my teenagers: Kids need clear directions and boundaries. Deep down they like authoritative commands and well-defined expectations. The more specific I am in dealing with my kids, the more they respond satisfactorily. For example, if I say, "After dinner tonight I would like for you to do your homework and take a shower. If you have time, clean your room and then you can play some." Thirty minutes later I am repeating myself for them to do what I have asked. Finally, when I specifically state my command to them, "You will do your homework now, then take a shower, and be in bed at 9:00 sharp," they hop to it.

When my commands are unclear, they are unsure of what to do. But when they are clear and spoken with authority, they understand and follow directions. (Most of the time.)

Throughout the Bible we read about God's callings for his people. His command to Jacob was clear. He said, "Go." He did not say, "Hey Jacob, if you feel like it, if you think you can, if you don't mind, if you have the time, how about going to Bethel and live there?" God says, "Go!"

Feeling unclear and uncertain about a decision in your life? Do you think God is calling you to make a change or improve what you are doing or is He telling you to continue as you are? Ask yourself, "Am I receiving an authoritative command from God? Is it clear?" If not, then continue praying about your life. Ask God for a clear command. If you think a calling is unclear and murky, then I would seriously question where the calling is coming from.

True callings from God are authoritative commands. Our God is not a God of ambiguity or confusion; He is a powerful, loving, and authoritative God.

1 Corinthians 14:33 "God is not a God of confusion but a God of peace." (NCV)

Part 5 – A Great Promise

Genesis 15:5 "Then the LORD brought Abram outside beneath the night sky and told him, 'Look up into the heavens and count the stars if you can. Your descendants will be like that-too many to count!'" (NLT)

My mom and dad went on a two-week trip to Europe. They celebrated both their 70th birthdays and their 50th wedding anniversary during this trip. They bought books, visited travel agents, and talked with friends who had been there and were like little children waiting for school to end for the summer. They had great expectations and great promises that the trip would be all they hoped for and more. It was interesting for me to see them transformed and renewed with energy over this trip. They seemed alive again and full of enthusiasm for life itself. I don't know if their expectations were met, but I do know that God will always honor His promises.

When God calls us, there is always a great promise made with the calling. In Genesis 12 when God calls Abram to leave his country and go to the land He would show him, God also made a promise to Abram. He promised Abram that he would be the father of a great nation. As we read through Genesis and follow Abram on his journey, we can see that his faith, hope, and life all center on God's promise. This promise was the motivating reason in all of Abram's decisions.

Think about it: God is not going to call you to do something just for the fun of it. God has a plan for your life. All of God's callings in your life have a promise with that calling. His promise is to be a loving Father and to provide for all our needs, wherever He leads us.

I often struggle with the promise part of a calling. Most people do. Think about it for a moment. Try to picture a calling God has in your life. What is keeping you from acting on that call? Is it the promise from God? Are you saying, "Yeah God, I hear Your call, but I just don't know if I can do that."

Let's take the most basic call in all of our lives, the call for obedience to God. He is such a loving God, that He wants to give us abundant life. We often think, "But I have to give up so much to be obedient." We do not focus on what we are gaining. It's like the alcoholic that just cannot imagine life without that next drink. He clings to his destructive behavior because he doesn't believe there is much to gain by giving up, letting go, and seeking the help he needs to end his self-destructive ways.

Have you heard the promise that goes with your calling? More importantly, are you listening to the promise? Even more importantly, do you trust the promise? Do you trust God? Do your trust Him with your life? God's tests in our lives are simply Him asking, "Do you trust Me?"

The promise gives us hope and hope gives us faith and belief in the calling. If you lose sight of the promise, you lose hope and then you lose faith in God.

In the above Scripture God is answering Abram's question about His promise to him. God is reassuring Abram about the promise. It is okay to question God, folks. It is okay to ask specific questions of God. It is okay to shout out to God that you don't understand, you don't hear, you don't listen, or that you don't want to do something. It's okay to be specific in your crying out to God about your calling. Even Jesus, before He was crucified, prayed to the Father, "Take this cup from Me." Jesus was questioning the call, but agreed to His Father's will in the end, not his own. How about you?

Part 6 – Change

Deuteronomy 1:6-7 "When we were at Mount Sinai, the LORD our God said to us, 'You have stayed at this mountain long enough.

It is time to break camp and move on.'" (NLT)

When temperatures plummet during the spring, I drape sheets over the trees and ornamental plants that have budded out, to protect them from the sudden change in weather. When God has a calling in our lives, He places a hedge around us to protect us and guide us along the way. Unlike my plants, we can still make our own decisions, which may be contrary to God's plan for us. However, whether we do it our way or God's way, He remains faithful to us.

Do you go around seeking change in your life? Do you like change? I have found that most of us do not enjoy it. Change brings stress, confusion, and fear into our lives. But God also uses change in our lives to propel us toward His callings.

Change is the fifth characteristic of a calling from God in your life. Think about this for a moment. When we seek to earnestly follow God and He intercepts our paths, change is the evidence of this interception. Sometimes we are moving in one direction toward a goal that is ours and not God's. Then God, through whatever means, redirects us along the way toward His plan for our lives.

Sometimes change involves God redirecting us within a calling. He wants us in a particular situation awhile until it's time for Him to move us again. I call these "seasons of preparation." God is simply preparing us for the next phase of our calling. The direction we were going in was within God's will, but now He is moving us farther along to another place in the calling. The big question remains: How do I know if it is God calling me to change my direction, or if it is just my own desire?

The summary below will help you out:

All callings from God are direct one-to-one callings in the first person. You will never hear God's callings unless you are where God has already called you.

All callings from God have clear direction. If we are moving in the direction that God has called us, He will continue to move us in that direction. Where God guides, God provides.

All callings from God are in the form of authoritative

commands. God is not a God of ambiguity or confusion.

All callings from God have a great promise attached. This promise gives us hope, hope gives us faith, and faith gives us belief in the calling.

All callings involve change. If you are moving in a direction contrary to God's plan for your life, He will intercept your direction and move you toward His plan. God will never move you in a direction that is contrary to His Word.

The prophet Jeremiah prays a great prayer, a model prayer for all of us today. Constantly pour your hearts out to God, asking for His guidance.

Jeremiah 10:23-24 "I know, LORD, that a person's life is not his own. No one is able to plan his own course. So correct me, LORD, but please be gentle. Do not correct me in anger, for I would die." (NLT)

Chapter 3

Drifting Away

Hebrews 2:1 "We must pay more careful attention, therefore, to what we have heard, so that we do not drift away." (NIV)

Folks, it's confession time. There are times I sometimes drift away from my relationship with God. Early on in my Christian life, like many, I had huge swings between being close and being distant from God. After twenty-five years of trying to "walk the talk," I have enjoyed experiencing fewer dramatic swings. The lows have been higher than the last low and the highs have been higher than the previous highs. So what made the difference? And how did I begin my recovery to a solid relationship with God?

Our relationship with Christ takes work, just as all our relationships do. We work at our marriages and friendships. We cannot build a new friendship, or preserve an old one, if we simply ignore the responsibilities that come with the territory. Trust, communication, unconditional love, time, and other fundamental foundations build successful marriages and friendships. Ignore one or more of these building blocks and watch the marriage or friendships slowly erode away.

Often in marriages, our lives go something like this: Marry, buy a house, climb the typical ladder of success, do volunteer work, have a kid or two, watch kids grow up, and then watch kids leave home. One day you look across the breakfast table and think, "Who is that person?" Over the years you drift apart, but it never is intentional. No one walks down the church aisle thinking, "Boy, I can't wait until we drift apart and get divorced. . ." Likewise, as Christians, we never thought, "Well, starting today, I am going to drift away from God."

So, what happens? The evil one's most effective tool to make me ineffective as a Christian is busyness. And doggone it, I know that, but I fall into the trap again and again. I feel like Paul when he said, "I do the things I know I should not do, and I don't do the things that I know I should do."

As I trace back over my steps, I hope you can learn from my failures. Three new business ventures were posed to me in one week. And in my sinful, carnal self, I thought that I could handle at least one more project, one more deal, and one more responsibility. My quiet time with God at night was shoved aside first. I took that time to pour myself into learning all I could about these ventures. I was reading every article and book I could find on the subjects. Of course, that cut into my Bible reading and prayer time. Then slowly, I became filled with some spiritual pride. My pride was telling me that I did not need to go to that Bible study this week or to the church service on the weekend.

Do not miss the point: I never intended to drift away; it was a gradual drift.

I love floating on rafts with my kids at the beach. Sometimes we look up and we have floated blocks away from where we entered the water. The current just slowly moved us, and we never knew we were drifting.

So what brought me back? The Holy Spirit within me kept nudging me back. I felt empty, without focus and purpose. Christian friends around me were asking me pointed questions: "Been reading your Bible everyday for you, and not just reading to write a devotional?" "When are you coming back to church?" "Do you still go to our church?" I am sure the small group of close people around me was prompted by the Holy Spirit to prod me back. Slowly I began to make time to pray and to read God's Word every day.

I guess we often wander away from God without realizing it, just like the current taking us down from our entry point. Maybe we just step out a short distance; maybe we go far away. The one fact I do know is that He is always waiting for us to come back. My favorite passage on this leaving and coming back is Luke 15:17-20,

"When he came to his senses, he said, "How many of my father's hired men have food to spare, and here I am starving to death! I will set out and go back to my father and say to him: Father, I have sinned against heaven and against you. I am no longer worthy to be called your son; make me like one of your hired men. So he got up and went to his father. But while he was still a long way off, his father saw him and was filled with compassion for him. He ran to his son, threw his arms around him and kissed him." (NIV)

It sure is nice to be back home.

Chapter Four

The Prodigal Son

Part 1 – Give Me

The story of the prodigal son is one of the best recognized parables in the Bible. It is my personal favorite. For both Christians and non-Christians, this is an applicable story for today. Follow with me as we journey alongside the prodigal son and retrace the footprints of our own life journeys over his footprints. We will walk slowly, careful not to miss our Savior's teaching. Come, let's take a walk together.

Luke 15:12-12 "Then he said, 'There was once a man who had two sons. The younger said to his father, Father, I want right now what's coming to me.'" (The Message)

"Give me." From birth throughout life, our human nature screams out, "Give me!" Our hyper-speed, technological society wants everything right now. We crave instant gratification for our wants. But have you noticed the more quickly you are satisfied, the faster you lose that joy? Instant satisfaction is like a drug. "Quick—give me another fix!"

In my profession as a real estate appraiser, I have the unique opportunity to go into people's homes and meet a wide, cross-section of people in my community. From the seemingly wealthy to the struggling laborers, I have seen the effects of the quick-fix attitude of instant gratification at some of these homes. (Not all home loans are bad.) I have witnessed the damage done by the give-it-to-me-now attitude. I have seen the abuse of credit cards and easy loans shatter families with stress fractures. The saddest appraisal experience for me is doing an appraisal on a repossessed home. Especially when I see children's toys still scattered about the house. I am amazed at the despair and despondency in some people's eyes as I enter their homes, after seeing all the grown-up toys outside. Inside, photos of cruises and trips to exotic places line the walls. Outside, two new cars, a boat, jet skis, the latest riding mower and other stuff clutter up the yard, but worse—they destroy their lives. I listen as some tell me that their home has to appraise for "this much" so they can pay off their five or six credit cards that are up to the limits. I just think to myself, "For the next thirty years, you are going to be paying for that Jet Ski, that trip to Disney World, that 'one more fix of instant gratification' that never lasted." More often than not, the home loan is not enough to cover the credit card and finance company debt.

The prodigal son story, told by Jesus two thousand years ago, has not changed. The son is saying to his father, "Give it to me now! Give me now what is going to be mine later." I am a patient, methodical, and calculating person, and I often find myself thinking, "Well one more deal, one more gain in the stock market, one more something, and everything will be all right." Our sinful human natures drive us like that. "Give me one more and all will be okay." It's the when-and-then attitude. "When I get that promotion, then we will be set," "When we buy this new car, then we will have made it." As Christians, we know the only thing human beings need is a gift that is free. Our problem is accepting the gift and using the power of the gift. A relationship with Christ is the craving we seek; it is a need that will never be filled by anything or anyone else.

The prodigal had the same attitude, "Father, give me what is mine now and watch what I can do apart from you." Or the attitude is, "Thanks for Christ and for him saving me, God—but I'll take it from here." In part two we will look at what the Father does and then the results of the son's journey apart from the Father.

Let's get out of the "give me" mode and into the "take me" mode with God.

Part 2 – I Want It Now!

Luke 15:14 "So the father divided the property between them. It wasn't long before the younger son packed his bags and left for a distant country. There, undisciplined and dissipated, he wasted everything he had." (The Message)

In part one of this chapter we focused on the younger son's "give me" attitude and his "when and then" attitude. Now we will follow the results of his "give it to me now" attitude.

Surprisingly, the father granted the son his request for his early inheritance. It is interesting that the son went to a distant land. He wanted nothing to do with his family; he wanted to be on his own. I am sure the son was riding sky high with anticipation of his new-found freedom. I can imagine him rubbing his hands with greed, pride, and false freedom from the rules and boundaries set by his father.

In our own lives, when all is seemingly going well, we have the tendency to think, "Okay God, thanks for the gift; now I will take it from here." Just as the son did with his father, we sometimes enter a phase of rebellion against God. My biggest stage of rebellion came when I went away from home to college. Perhaps a crisis in your life drives you away from God and into your own "distant land." We are deceived into thinking that we have freedom apart from God, when in fact we become slaves to sin. Away from God, we have the same rebellious spirit as the younger son.

Many people have told me that they want nothing to do with the church or Christ. They don't want to accept God's rules because they are scared of what God may ask them to give up. What they miss is the huge gain that God's protective boundaries give us. Living by God's plan frees us from much of the pain the younger son went through apart from God.

When apart from the father, the son became undisciplined and dissipated. I can imagine the son going to the local tavern and buying rounds of drinks for everyone, thinking he was gaining true friends and happiness. His wild living was spent on sinful, temporal pleasures. I am sure he probably tried to fulfill his insatiable need for instant satisfaction with sex, drugs, materialistic items, and other sinful means.

John 15:5 "I am the vine; you are the branches. If a man remains in me and I in him, he will bear much fruit; apart from me you can do nothing." (NIV)

Apart from Christ we can do nothing that bears fruit. Apart from Christ, the younger son wasted everything (Luke 15:14). Apart from Christ, I waste things. I waste money, I waste time, I waste good memories, and I waste His blessings that He gives out to those who are walking in close fellowship with Him.

Let's keep following the prodigal son. In part three, we will follow him to the bottom of his journey. Let's pray for God's wisdom and for us to keep growing closer to Him so that we don't waste the life He has given us. Let's pray that we will search out areas in our life where we are rebelling against God and start reveling in Him. Let's not miss His blessings.

Part 3 – The Bottom

Luke 15:14-16 "After he had gone through all his money, there was a bad famine all through that country and he began to hurt. He signed on with a citizen there who assigned him to his fields to slop the pigs. He was so hungry he would have eaten the corncobs in the pig slop, but no one would give him any." (The Message)

As we journey with the prodigal son, we have seen him go from being discontent with his home, to entering an instant gratification stage of "give it to me now." This led to a rebellious stage of "I can do it all on my own." Now we continue to see the outcomes of the son's poor choices. While our Father in Heaven has given us the freedom to make choices on our own, He has not given us the alternative to choose the results of those choices.

I still imagine the son going to this distant land, trying to impress people and buying friends with his money. I see him buying rounds of drinks in the bar, buying the latest designer sandals and robes, buying sexual and other illicit favors. As we say here in the South, he was living in "high cotton." He thought, as many of us think today, that money was the answer to all his needs. On top of his money running out, the country went into a famine, or in modern terms a recession. Where were his newfound friends now? Can you see the son going up to some of his bar buddies and saying, "Hey, remember me? Can you get me a job at your tent shop?" "Remember all I bought you guys?" But clearly his friends evaporated as quickly as his money.

Jesus tells us the son began to hurt, but he was still in denial. His denial was lying to himself about his true condition. Often our denial leads us to self-destructive behavior. We may turn to alcohol, drugs, pornography, or become immersed in our work to escape the pains of slipping out of denial. The prodigal son was lying to himself about the results of his own actions. Although he was hurting, he still thought he was in control. He still was not thinking of his home. So he took the lowest job—probably the only job he could find, thinking that this, too, was just a crisis that he could overcome on his own.

Finally his hurting overcame his delusion and turned his thoughts back to home. His hurting made him realize that he had needs that he alone could not fulfill.

Luke 15:17 "That brought him to his senses. He said, 'All those farmhands working for my father sit down to three meals a day, and here I am starving to death.'" (The Message)

What a wonderful verse. When he finally hit his low point, he came to his senses. He came out of his denial and became keenly aware of his predicament. How many of us need to come out of denial—come out of lying to ourselves about our lives—and come to our senses? When do we finally say, "Enough is enough of this way I am living? Enough is enough of this running from what I know God wants from me." When do we yield to God's plan and His love for us? When do we admit that apart from Him we are living out of control? Are you yet sick and tired of being sick and tired of your actions?

The son remembered how well his father treated his farmhands. They had seemed menial to the son, but now they seemed wealthy. The father treated them with respect and love. They had all their needs met.

There is so much to learn from this parable. Now we see the son begin to be in want. This want leads to him to reflect on his life, which in turn leads him out of denial. What part or parts of your life are you in denial about and need to reflect on? Maybe it is your job. Perhaps it is your keeping up with the Jones' lifestyle and living beyond your means. Is it your relationship with your classmates at school or your teachers? How about your relationship with your parents and other family members? Are you trying to live apart from God? Still running from what you know God is calling you to do? Still denying your own faults and sins? Join me in stepping back, slowing down, and reflecting on life.

Let's get moving from denial to reflection.

Part 4 – Reflection

Luke 15:18-19 "I'm going back to my father. I'll say to him, 'Father, I've sinned against God, I've sinned before you; I don't deserve to be called your son. Take me on as a hired hand.'" (The Message)

As hunger pains hit his stomach, and the stench of pigs permeated his entire body, he realized his predicament. We see the son go from reflecting on his life to resolving to go back to his father and confess his sins.

Often we become mired down in the muck of the outcomes of our sinful actions. We become paralyzed with guilt and constricted by the pains we have caused not only others, but also ourselves. We may go through a stage of anger at the world. Anger directed inward at ourselves can lead to depression. I see the prodigal son sitting in a pigsty, thinking only of himself and his problems, having a pity party of one.

Only when he begins to focus his thoughts outward, does the solution to his problem become obvious. Like a light bulb in a darkroom, his mind and his expression light up with hope. He finally admits to himself that he has sinned. He and only he can begin the journey back to his father and home. You and only you can make a conscious decision to turn away from the direction you are going and turn back toward God—toward our home.

When resolving to go back, we now get the "big picture" of the parable. The son remembers the loving home of his father. Pigs are comfortable in their pigpens, but we humans don't like being outside our true home—Our Father's home—where we were made in His image. A home where He is watching out for us. A home where He is always faithful to us.

Luke 15:20 "He got right up and went home to his father." (The Message)

His resolution to go home leads him to repentance. This parable draws a beautiful picture of the meaning of repentance. Repentance is not simply saying, "Hey, God—I am sorry for sinning." True repentance is not only being sorry for our sins, but it also includes turning away from those sins. Just as the son now turns away from his sinful direction in life, we should turn away from the sinful lures waiting for us when we go down the road of life in the wrong direction.

Turning away from a sinful life often involves turning away from people in our lives that are pulling us down with them. A person with a drug addiction wants you to be addicted with him. A person with a pornography problem wants you to go with him to the adult bookstore or the topless bar. Sinners love company. It makes them feel better about themselves. We do it; we look at others and set standards for ourselves. We kid ourselves about our own problems by looking at others and thinking, "Well, David drinks a lot, so it is all right for me to do the same." We are simply rationalizing away our sinful ways, just as a child uses rationalization to justify his wrong actions.

Examine your life, and then resolve to return to your Heavenly Father and take action in any areas where you need to repent.

In part five we will follow the son home. We will see his resolution turn into a restoration with his father and his life that he left behind.

Part 5 – Restoration

Jesus now tells us the most beautiful part of this parable, the restoration of the son and father. I surmise the son plodding toward home, with his feet shuffling and his shoulders sagging. His clothes are reeking of the smell of pigs. His designer sandals are muddy and worn. His palms are sweating as he is rehearsing his repentance speech over and over in his dejected mind.

Luke 15:20a-21 "When he was still a long way off, his father saw him. His heart pounding, he ran out, embraced him, and kissed him. The son started his speech: "Father, I've sinned against God, I've sinned before you; I don't deserve to be called your son ever again." (The Message)

The father knew his son would return one day. He waited patiently, straining his eyes every day as he scanned the horizon, hoping to see his son coming home. The father's love for his son never waned—he was still his son. Now notice what the father does when the son starts his long-rehearsed repentance speech. The father does not do what we expect. He does not call out for his best whip to give the son a lashing. He does not start screaming, yelling, and chastising the son. The father reacts counter intuitively to how most of us would react to a prodigal son or daughter that has squandered not only money but also the family name. The father interrupts the son's speech:

Luke 15:22 "But the father wasn't listening. He was calling to the servants, 'Quick. Bring a clean set of clothes and dress him. Put the family ring on his finger and sandals on his feet.'" (The Message)

The father reacted with compassion and love for the son. The father had allowed the son to go on his odyssey to the land far off. The father knew the son had a tough lesson to learn—one that could only be learned by experience. Sometimes I allow my own children to make decisions that I know will not be good for them, because sometimes they need to learn things on their own. But when my kids do things that displease me, I don't disown them. I can never change the fact that they are my children. My love for them is unconditional, just as the father's love for the prodigal is unconditional.

We Christians sometimes fall into a life a sin. We are human beings and we are not perfect. Many commentators and preachers see this parable as an example of a person who has never accepted Christ as his Savior. I have to disagree and say that it is a parable about Christians, children of God, who have stumbled and are living a sinful life apart from God. We can choose a lifestyle of sin apart from our Heavenly Father, but we cannot enjoy this life.

Every day, our Father in Heaven looks for us to come back home. He waits patiently for us to come back and return to fellowship with Him. When we mess up, He embraces us with compassion and wraps us in His love, the love that we often don't feel when we are in our "pigpens" of life. A friend of mine recently said, "God needs to show up at my front door with a dozen roses."

I said, "No, you need to go back home to God. He is waiting. Ready to embrace you, ready to wash off your filthy garments of sin and make you clean again."

Some people have told me, "God could never love me with all the bad I have done." None of our sins are unknown to God. Nothing we have done or will do is a surprise to God. He is eagerly waiting for you to come back home. God is not waiting for you to come back so He can beat you down some more. He is not sitting on His throne, waiting for the opportunity to scold you. You have done that on your own. God is waiting for you so He can embrace you and love you. Are you ready to go back?

1 John 1:9 "On the other hand, if we admit our sins—make a clean break of them—he won't let us down; he'll be true to Himself. He'll forgive our sins and purge us of all wrongdoing." (The Message)

Part 6 – Homecoming

Luke 15:25-27 "All this time his older son was out in the field. When the day's work was done he came in. As he approached the house, he heard the music and dancing. Calling over one of the houseboys, he asked what was going on. He told him, 'Your brother came home. Your father has ordered a feast—barbecued beef!—because he has him home safe and sound.' The older brother stalked off in an angry sulk and refused to join in." (The Message)

Ever felt like the older brother? I have. When we were growing up, my two older brothers were always getting into trouble. Seeing them in hot water was a deterrent for me to try to stay out of serious mischief, myself. Or perhaps I was just good at not getting caught!

Let's get honest with each other. How many times have you looked at another family member, co-worker, neighbor, classmate, or friend, and had feelings of jealousy and anger come over you? Like the older brother, you and I sulk and fume because we feel like we are doing everything right, while they live far outside the foul lines—yet they suffer no adverse effects. I know I have done this. I scream at God, "Hey God, what about me? What about all the good I am doing? Where are my blessings, God?"

Let's eavesdrop on the older son:

Luke 15:29-30 "The son said, 'Look how many years I've stayed here serving you, never giving you one moment of grief, but have you ever thrown a party for me and my friends? Then this son of yours who has thrown away your money on whores shows up and you go all out with a feast!'" (The Message)

The older son is the other lost son in this parable. It should be titled, "Two Lost Sons." The younger son was lost in his sinful living; the older son was lost in his pride. The younger son was lost far away from his father; the older son was lost at home. Both were equally apart from and out of fellowship with their father. I have heard church members say of people that have never been to church, "Those people need to clean up their act, put on their Sunday best, learn our songs and our creeds, and then come to our church." If you think like that, you have it as backwards as trying to catch fish already cleaned. You have to catch the fish first. I find it interesting that the Father went out to the older son and pleaded with him to come inside the home. In the same way we need to go outside the walls of church and into the fields, to the lost people of our world.

Luke 15:31-32 "His father said, 'Son, you don't understand. You're with me all the time, and everything that is mine is yours—but this is a wonderful time, and we had to celebrate. This brother of yours was dead, and he's alive! He was lost, and he's found!'" (The Message)

The older brother never lost anything while the younger son was gone. The older brother received his inheritance in advance, just as the younger son had. The older brother had much more than an inheritance under his belt. He had the joy of living and being with his father daily. But his spiritual pride and his self-centeredness prevented him from recognizing the great blessings around him.

So where are you in the parable? I bounce around from being the younger son to being the older son—wandering away from home at times, and at other times wanting everything to myself while I am home. Our goal is to be like the third son—the narrator of the parable. The third son, Christ, is our model. Our Heavenly Father is no different from these boys' dad. He is a loving and just Father, wanting nothing more from us than ourselves. Through the power of the Holy Spirit, we can strive to be like Christ, and in turn we have a right relationship with our Father in Heaven.

We need to be more sensitive to those that are prodigals around us, both people who do not know the love of God and people who have wandered from the faith. If you are one of these lost people, I pray that you will come home or back home. If you were lost, stop beating yourself up and fully enjoy the blessings in our home. If you are like the older brother in the story, I pray you will stop looking inward and start looking outward to the lost people around you. Reach out to them and help bring them home.

Chapter 5

Spiritual Disciplines

Part 1 – Introduction

When my son Bobby was four I took him to a Duke University Basketball game. We arrived 30 minutes early so he could see the players practicing and warming up. The players started out dribbling the ball and taking some easy lay-up shots. Over the 30-minute period they progressed to more difficult but fundamental skills. Bobby excitedly enjoyed watching the practice, but at one point he looked up and said, "Dad, where is the other team?" I told him they would be out in a few minutes and then the game would begin, that right now the players were preparing for the battle. After the game started Bobby said, "Dad, they sure are playing better now!"

Isn't that what we need to be doing? We need to be practicing our fundamentals, preparing for battle, getting the basics right, and growing in our faith. We will never get better, stronger, and closer without the fundamentals. Let's take a practical look at spiritual disciplines, our workouts that help us become more like Christ.

What are spiritual disciplines? To me they are the following: Bible reading, prayer, fasting, worship, stewardship, serving, silence, writing a journal, and growing in knowledge. You may have others.

You might be thinking, "Gee David, this sounds great but why bother?" Walk with me back in time. Let's take a quick journey back to a trial that occurred nearly 2000 years ago.

Matthew 27:16-22 "At that time they had a notorious prisoner, called Barabbas. So when the crowd had gathered, Pilate asked them, 'Which one do you want me to release to you: Barabbas, or Jesus who is called Christ?' For he knew it was out of envy that they had handed Jesus over to him. While Pilate was sitting on the judge's seat, his wife sent him this message: 'Don't have anything to do with that innocent man, for I have suffered a great deal today in a dream because of him.' But the chief priests and the elders persuaded the crowd to ask for Barabbas and to have Jesus executed. 'Which of the two do you want me to release to you?' asked the governor. 'Barabbas,' they answered. 'What shall I do, then, with Jesus who is called Christ?' Pilate asked. They all answered, 'Crucify him!'" (The Message)

Do you realize who Barabbas is? He represents you and I. We belonged on that cross. We deserved to die that horrible death. We should have been there. So it should be out of our gratitude to Christ for dying in our place, that we work toward being more like Christ.

Ephesians 2:8-10 (NIV) "For it is by grace you have been saved, through faith, and this not from yourselves, it is the gift of God, not by works, so that no one can boast. For we are God's workmanship, created in Christ Jesus to do good works, which God prepared in advance for us to do."

Part 2 – Bible Reading

Do you read instruction manuals? Are you like me when you buy a new computer program? I have never read how to use or install the programs! I just stick the disk or the CD in the correct drive and type setup. The only time I go to the instruction book is when problems arise and that can be often! Lately I have discovered my life with computers is much more congenial when I read the instructions first.

You know God has given us an instruction manual. I love the acronym for B.I.B.L.E., "Basic Instructions Before Leaving Earth". It's all written down for us in one convenient place. Simply put, the Bible teaches us how to do life right. It sure is easier to read God's instructions first, and then act. But so often we act, then run to the Bible to figure out how to get out of the mess we have created in our lives.

Psalm 119:9-11 (NIV) "How can a young man keep his way pure? By living according to your word. I seek you with all my heart; do not let me stray from your commands. I have hidden your word in my heart that I might not sin against you."

The psalmist hid the Word in his heart so that he could do life right.

2 Timothy 3:16-17 (NIV) *"All Scripture is God-breathed and is useful for teaching, rebuking, correcting and training in righteousness, so that the man of God may be thoroughly equipped for every good work."* Notice Paul doesn't say, "Some Scripture is useful" or "Pick the parts you like to use". Paul says *"all Scripture" is useful."*

One of the first questions I ask folks when they come to me with a crisis is "How often are you reading God's Word?"

Most will say, "Well gee David, you see, with this crisis, I just have not been reading the Bible, in fact I have not been reading it much during the past few months or years." Then usually they will say "But I am going to start real soon!" We have it backwards folks, you have to read the instructions first, and then apply them to your life. You have to move what you learn from the Bible from your head, to your heart, and finally to your feet.

Ezra 7:10 (NIV) "For Ezra had devoted himself to the study and observance of the Law of the LORD, and to teaching its decrees and laws in Israel."

Matthew 4:4 (NIV) *"Jesus answered, 'It is written: 'Man does not live on bread alone, but on every word that comes from the mouth of God.'" John 17:17 (NIV) "Sanctify them by the truth; your word is truth."* I want to look at some practical, yet simple ways to get into reading the Bible, which have helped me. Of course, what works for me, may not work for you. It took me years of trying to figure out a way to ensure that I read the Bible everyday. The key to doing it is growing in Christ. Loving Christ so much, and being so appreciative for what He did for us on the cross nearly 2000 years ago, that we naturally thirst and hunger for His Word, His truth.

The first step I recommend is getting a version of the Bible with which you feel comfortable. I nearly failed English Literature in college because I had a hard time with Old English. We have a wealth of translations available. Take the time to find one that is right for you. I often read paraphrased editions such as The Message and The New Living Bible. They are wonderful for reading, but I do not recommend them for serious Bible study. I prefer the New Living Translation, and gain much insight from finding the original Hebrew or Greek words.

Ideas for Daily Reading

1. Set a time during the day for reading the Bible. Make an "appointment" with God and keep it. I am a morning person and love immersing in the Word before the kids wake up, and before getting bogged down in my hectic daily work. Have a plan and follow your plan.

2. Daily devotional guides are an excellent way to start. Most churches have these available. Some good ones are Guideposts, Daily Bread, and Moody has a good one called Today's Word.

3. Read the Bible to your children. I have learned much from reading children's Bible stories to my kids. The obvious added benefit is showing your children how important God's Word is to your family. My daughters now read their Bibles every night before bed. It has become a habit with them.

4. Buy a version of the Bible on cassette tapes. I often listen to God's Word in my car or while exercising. I have also found my

mind cluttered and I have trouble concentrating. Listening to the tape and following along in the Bible will propel my reading to where it needs to be.

5. Buy a "One-Year Bible" arranged in daily reading that will take you through God's Word in twelve months. These Bibles come in various versions and arranged in a logical manner.

6. Find a partner and do a topical Bible study together. For me, this has been a rewarding way to read the Bible. The neat part is the built-in accountability you have by having a partner.

7. Join a Bible study group or better yet, if you have the ability to teach, start one. I have learned more, and concentrate more on my reading, by teaching. The adage "The best way to learn is to teach" is so true.

Part 3 – Prayer

Luke 18:1 "Then Jesus told his disciples a parable to show them that they should always pray and not give up." (NIV)

Colossians 4:2 "Devote yourselves to prayer, being watchful and thankful." (NIV)

When you think of prayer, what do you think about? I used to think prayer was for spiritual people, the kind who can pray eloquently in public. I believed there was a formula—a certain procedure—and only one correct way to pray. In short, prayer was intimidating to me. Years ago, I heard the following true story and it changed my prayer life from that day on.

A pastor of a large church in a Midwest town received a phone call from a lady who was distraught. This lady had been taking care of her elderly father in her home for several years. Her father was unable to get out of bed, and she had to care for all his physical needs—but he was mentally alert. It seems the father had heard the pastor on the radio for the past several years, and had become fond of his teaching. The daughter told the pastor that her father wanted to meet with him, as they were unchurched and had no pastor to call on. The pastor went to the daughter's house and was led down the hall to the father's bedroom. The kind elderly gentleman's face beamed upon meeting the pastor, as he invited him to sit down and chat. As the pastor moved toward a wooden ladder-back chair to sit down, the gentleman said, "Umm... sorry pastor, no one can sit in that chair; please sit over here." The pastor thought that was odd until the man said, "You see, pastor, that chair is for Jesus. When I pray, Jesus is sitting in that chair, and we have conversations. I pray, and then I listen for the quiet, still voice of our Lord."

That hit me between the eyes. Prayer is a conversation with our Lord. No fancy fluff, no rules, no boundaries—just simple conversation.

Psalm 62:8 "Trust in him at all times, O people; Pour out your hearts to him, for God is our refuge." (NIV)

A few weeks later, the pastor received a phone call from the daughter, saying her father had died, and she asked him to serve at the funeral. As she was hanging up, she said, "You know, pastor, my dad died in a strange way. We found him kneeling down, with his head lying in that old wooden chair."

Samuel Chadwick once said, "The one concern of the Devil is to keep Christians from praying. He fears nothing from prayerless studies, prayerless work, and prayerless religion. He laughs at our toil, mocks at our wisdom, but trembles when we pray."

John 16:24 (NKJV) "Jesus said, *"Until now you have asked nothing in My name. Ask, and you will receive, that your joy may be full."* Jesus expects us to pray. He placed a high priority on prayer. In the NIV translation, prayer or praying is mentioned 226 times. Why is praying so hard? I have to believe it is hard because praying is not a "natural" human design. All our lives we are taught to be self-sufficient. We have a God that loves us much and wants us to pour our hearts out to Him often—through prayer.

Psalm 62:8 "Trust in him at all times, O people; Pour out your hearts to him, for God is our refuse." (NIV)

Simple Ideas for a Better Prayer Life

1. Make a daily appointment with God and keep it. Set at least one time during the day to talk to God. Make prayer a top priority in your life.
2. If you have children, pray with them before they go to school. I also love praying with my kids at night after we talk about their day. Let them see that prayer is a priority in your life.
3. Pray with you spouse. Pray for each other and express your thanks and needs to God.
4. Use what a friend of mine calls "bullet" prayers. Short prayers all during the day. I love these prayers while waiting at stoplights, in grocery store lines, while getting gas, and other idle times during the day.
5. Find someone to be your prayer partner. Hold each other accountable for praying and pray together. Many prayer partners exist on the Internet and by email.
6. Use a prayer journal. Write down your prayers. Go back and write how God has heard your prayers. You will be amazed at the effectiveness of prayer journals. Years ago writing my prayers was the only way I could focus long enough to complete a prayer.
7. Go for walks and pray. Imagine God walking along and listening to you.
8. My favorite tip is this. Pick a chair like the gentleman in the preceding story and close your eyes and imagine Jesus sitting there. Just talk and pray to Him. He loves to hear what is on your heart. I have several "chairs" for Jesus—one at home, one here at the office, and of course He loves riding in the car with me. I love praying out loud to Him in the car. Yes, I get some funny looks from other motorists!

Part 4 – Use a Spiritual Journal

Psalm 143:5 (NIV) "I remember the days of long ago; I meditate on all your works and consider what your hands have done. I spread out my hands to you; my soul thirsts for you like a parched land. Selah"

Once after cleaning out a cabinet in my study, I came upon a baby book of my first child, Morgan. In this book there were lists of many of her "firsts". Her first tooth, first Christmas, first crawl, first walk, and even her first haircut was included! Morgan and I sat down and went through the book, and it was a thrill to reminisce about her early childhood. As we talked about all the highlights of her life until now, she enjoyed seeing and hearing about the journey of her life.

Likewise, a spiritual journal is simply a place to write down the adventures in your walk with God. This is an effective discipline by which you can hold yourself accountable for all the other disciplines, and it helps you preserve daily conversations with Jesus. There are no rules for journaling. If I had one rule, it would be to be honest in writing your thoughts down in the journal. God wants your heart.

Now you are probably thinking, "Great David. How do I do this?" Well, I have tried several different ways to journal. What works best for me is a simple diary, with the days of the year and blank pages. What do I write? A book I've found helpful in my journey is The Disciple's Journal, published by Narrow Road Publishing. This book is a great year-long Bible study and journaling tool. Unfortunately, this book is now out of print. Below are some prompts from the book:

Prompt ideas:
See Jesus sitting across from you. What would you say to Him? Write this down.
Write out one fact you are afraid to tell Jesus. Then tell Him why you have been afraid.
Meditate on a passage of Scripture, and write down questions or ideas about the passage that you do not understand.
Ask the Lord to tell you how you can know Him better and make this your purpose during the day. Write down His response to you; describe the experience.
Write down prayers and requests. Review these often and see how God has responded to your prayers.
Write down new insights you have gained from reading the Bible.

Write down anything related to your walk with Christ.

I encourage you to start a journal. If you are nervous about writing, remember that only you and God will ever see it. Just pray and start writing a little bit from your heart. The more you write, the more natural it will become.

Part 5 – Fasting

Fasting is a lost discipline for many people. There are few sermons on fasting today. I have found in teaching Bible studies that even the most seasoned Christians lack knowledge and understanding of fasting. Let's look at what Jesus said about fasting.

Matthew 6:16 "When you fast, do not look somber as the hypocrites do, for they disfigure their faces to show men they are fasting. I tell you the truth, they have received their reward in full." (NIV)

Jesus expects us to fast. He said, "When you fast" not "if you fast, when you feel like fasting, or if you are so inclined to fast." Notice, too, that Jesus did not say you must fast. Let's not become legalistic like the Pharisees and let's not be like the hypocrites who fasted for the wrong reasons.

Acts 13:2-3 "While they were worshipping the Lord and fasting, the Holy Spirit said, 'Set apart for me Barnabas and Saul for the work to which I have called them.' So after they had fasted and prayed, they placed their hands on them and sent them off." (NIV)

What then is the right reason to fast? Fasting should always be for spiritual purposes. Clearly the early church fasted, worshiped, and prayed. That, my friends, is the key to fasting. It should be a voluntary, private, worshipful, and a prayerful time between you and our heavenly Father.

My most successful fasts have been when I concentrated on one aspect, one want, one yearning, and one longing to be closer to God and to listen to His will for my life. For example, if I am reading the Bible and the Holy Spirit clearly clarifies a passage for me in a way that I can only describe as supernatural, I will fast and meditate on that passage during the entire fast.

I have also found great success in concentrating on one prayer during a fast. The prayer is usually a prayer of thanksgiving for what Christ has done for me, and one need that I pray God will grant to me. Again the key is to focus on Christ during the fast. Good fasts have always been life changing for me.

What's a bad fast? That is when I fast for the wrong reason or the wrong attitude in my heart. I have had fasts in which I never experienced the presence of God. Looking back I always was fasting without focusing on Christ during the fast.

So, how do you fast? I always suggest to people to start slow, and of course if you have any medical problems, consult your doctor before fasting. On that note, fasting can mean withholding anything you want; it does not have to mean an absence of food. So anyone can fast.

I recommend people start out with a 24-hour fast. This simply means skipping two meals—preferably breakfast and lunch. I do drink water during the fast; some folks drink fruit juice. There are no rules. During the day when the hunger pains occur, pray and focus on Christ and on your purpose for the fast. The pains always remind me of how helpless I am without God. He provides all my needs. There are several books on fasting. I recommend finding a good book and learning more about how to fast in a safe and spiritual way.

Part 6 – Solitude and Silence

Solitude and silence—great sounding words, neat idea, but are they practical and obtainable? We are bombarded with noise from the moment we wake up until we retire at night. Think about it. We wake up to a clock radio blaring, turn the TV on during breakfast, listen to more radio in the shower, and hop in the car with the cassette player or CD player going. Next, we enter our workplace with our minds racing about the urgencies awaiting us. Then it's back home again with a mind cluttered with noise. Where is God in all this? When do we have time to be still and know our Lord?

Solitude and silence are the key to all the spiritual disciplines. You can't effectively read your Bible, pray, or meditate without clearing out the clutter of noise—whether the noise is external noise or the internal noises of your mind. I am firmly convinced that distraction is one of the evil one's greatest tools to prevent us from becoming closer to God.

Matthew 14:23 (NIV) "After he had dismissed them, he went up on a mountainside by himself to pray. When evening came, he was there alone."

Mark 1:35 (NIV) "Very early in the morning, while it was still dark, Jesus got up, left the house and went off to a solitary place, where he prayed."

Luke 4:42 (NIV) "At daybreak Jesus went out to a solitary place. The people were looking for him and when they came to where he was, they tried to keep him from leaving them.

Psalm 62:1 (NIV) "My soul finds rest in God alone; my salvation comes from him." Isaiah 30:15 (NIV) "This is what the Sovereign LORD, the Holy One of Israel, says: 'In repentance and rest is your salvation, in quietness and trust is your strength.'"

The Bible is clear that God expects us to spend quiet time with Him in His presence. I have found it helpful to spend my solitude time with God in the morning. I go to the same room and the same chair every morning.

It is also helpful to take time during the day to have just five minutes of solitude whenever you can grab the time—in the car, in your office, at your desk in school, or wherever you may be. Just try to focus on Christ and clear the clutter from your mind. Let Christ renew you.

Chapter 6

Balancing the Gauges

~~~

Part 1 – Running Fast!

Ecclesiastics 4:44 "I realized the reason people work hard and try to succeed: They are jealous of each other. This, too, is useless, like chasing the wind." (NCV)

Ecclesiastics 4:6 "Maybe so, but I say it is better to be content with what little you have. Otherwise, you will always be struggling for more, and that is like chasing the wind." (NCV)

We live in a hectic, fast-paced world. Advertisements constantly bombard us with technology to make life simpler. Do life faster. Do life better. Do more, better and in less time. Well, you know what I have found out? The faster and more I can do things, the more people want and expect.

For example at work, I was the first real estate appraiser around to automate and the first in town with a digital camera. All the latest technology crams my office. I can crank out some work, folks! My thinking was, "Get a faster computer, better software, better, more bells and whistles, and then I will have more down time. I will have more time to study, write, minister and goof off." But you know what happened? The more work I did and the faster I did it, the more work my clients expected of me. I spoiled them! But, worse than that, I fell into a trap. The trap was the world sucking the life out of me—and it still does at times, when I let it. The world does not care about your physical, spiritual, or emotional health.

Nahun 2:4 "The chariots race through the streets and rush back and forth through the city squares. They look like torches; they run like lightning." (NCV)

Jeremiah 12:5 "If you have run with footmen and they have tired you out, then how can you compete with horses? If you fall down in a land of peace, how will you do in the thicket of the Jordan?" (NASB)

Do you ever start running so fast and so hard at work, home, or school that you push aside everything else? You shove past and walk over your relationships, family, and Christ. You stomp on the people you love, and go out of your way to please people who could care less about you. Think of your life as having a dashboard with gauges similar to your car. Your physical gauge is screaming for more sleep, exercise, and better eating habits. Your emotional gauge is redlining. You have reached your limit. You become short-tempered, forgetful, and self-centered. Your spiritual gauge rests on empty. You never make time for prayer, devotions, Bible study, or fellowship. Or when you do, you are so out of balanced that you can't focus on any of your spiritual disciplines. How do we get all our gauges back to being in balance?
 In my next four devotionals, I want look at some Biblical ways to manage and balance our emotional, spiritual, and physical gauges on our dashboard.
 We need to devote ourselves daily, worship weekly, measure monthly, and abandon yearly.

Part 2 – Devote Daily

Titus 3:8 "This is a trustworthy saying. And I want you to stress these things, so that those who have trusted in God may be careful to devote themselves to doing what is good. These things are excellent and profitable for everyone." (NIV)

Titus 3:14 "Our people must learn to devote themselves to doing what is good, in order that they may provide for daily necessities and not live unproductive lives." (NIV)

In part one I discussed the hectic pace of our world and how the fast-paced lifestyle of the world can play havoc on our emotional, physical, and spiritual gauges. This and the next three parts will build on my final statement in Part 1: Devote daily, worship weekly, measure monthly, and abandon annually. The questions pressing all of us as Christ-followers is, "How do I live in the world without becoming part of the world? How can I live life right as a Christian, with the world being so out-of-balance and so un-Christ like?" The world tugs hard on our hearts, minds, and bodies. The world wants to suck us in and spit us out like worthless pawns, used and toyed with for the benefit of others who could not give a rip about us as human beings.

What does it mean to devote ourselves daily? Let's look at the following verses.

Matthew 6:11 "Give us this day our daily bread." (NRSV)

First and foremost, prayer is essential to devoting daily. Prayer is so obvious, yet so few engage in sincere heartfelt and "heart poured out to God" prayer. Give us our daily portion of grace, Lord. Give us our daily measure of Your love. Give us our daily strength to continue in You, Father. As the nation of Israel wandered in the desert, the Lord provided them with manna. An interesting property of the manna was that it would only keep for one day, and each person had to gather his provision for the day. Fathers could not gather manna for the children; each had to daily gather his own.

And we must each gather daily our provision that God has laid out for us.

Luke 9:23 "Then he said to them all, 'If any want to become my followers, let them deny themselves and take up their cross daily and follow me.'" (NRSV)

We must daily—not weekly, not monthly, not yearly at a Christmas Eve service—take up our cross and follow Christ. We must deny ourselves, which simply means we must stop being self-centered and become Christ-centered each day.

Acts 17:11 "These Jews were more fair-minded than those in Thessalonica, for they received the word with all willingness and examined the scriptures daily to determine whether these things were so." (NIV)

What more can I add? They searched the Scriptures daily. They read the Bible daily. We must read the Bible daily. God put His word in the Bible for us to read and follow. Set aside at least one time each day to read the Bible. Make an appointment with God's Word, and keep it.

1 Thessalonians 4:12 "So that your daily life may win the respect of outsiders and so that you will not be dependent on anybody." (NIV)

Hebrews 3:13 "But exhort one another every day, as long as it is called 'today,' so that none of you may be hardened by the deceitfulness of sin." (NRSV)

Our "walk" each day, each moment, should represent our life in Christ. We are called to be different from the world. Your life should stand out, stand apart from the world. How do we do this? It's in the little things we do. It's each seemingly small decision we make each day—minute by minute. It is using God's wisdom, not the world's wisdom. It is stopping yourself before each decision, each thought, each word spoken, and each action taken and thinking, "Will this win the respect of others, will this glorify Christ, will this decision build up or tear down the Kingdom?" I call this living by M & M's. No not the candy! M & M stands for moment-by-moment living for Christ. Maturing in Christ is our moment-by-moment acceptance of God's wise provision of grace for us. Maturing is becoming more and more sensitive to the promptings of the Holy Spirit who lives in us, and acting on these promptings to bring Him glory.

Part 3 – Worship Weekly

Ephesians 5:18-20 "Do not get drunk with wine, for that is debauchery; but be filled with the Spirit, as you sing psalms and hymns and spiritual songs among yourselves, singing and making melody to the Lord in your hearts, giving thanks to God the Father at all times and for everything in the name of our Lord Jesus Christ." (NRSV)

Hebrews 10:25 "Let us not give up meeting together, as some are in the habit of doing, but let us encourage one another—and all the more as you see the Day approaching." (NIV)

Acts 20:7 "On the first day of the week, when we met to break bread, Paul was holding a discussion with them; since he intended to leave the next day, he continued speaking until midnight." (NRSV)

It helps me to balance my gauges by stopping at least once a week and worshiping our Holy God. The purpose of church is to worship God. I think that if you are not part of a local church, you are denying the body of Christ the opportunity to minister to you and to be ministered by you. God has uniquely wired each of us up in a special way, so together we can carry out His unique plan for our lives.

I was at the Billy Graham Training Center in Asheville, North Carolina a few months ago, taking a course on 1 Timothy. On the grounds is a beautiful chapel, and during the tour the question came up, "What time is the Sunday service?" The tour guide told us that Billy Graham is such a strong believer in the local church that he will not allow Sunday services in the chapel. That struck home to me, because I am a contributing member of a local church.

Below are four reasons I see for us to worship weekly. You may have other reasons as well.

Psalms 138:2 "I will worship toward Your holy temple, And praise Your name For Your loving kindness and Your truth; For You have magnified Your word above all Your name." (NKJV)

1. To Worship God. The church is a special place to humble ourselves before our Holy God, to praise Him, respect Him, and show our reverence to Him. The Greek word for worship literally means, "to kiss, like a dog licking a master's hand." Worship is blocking out the world around us and simply experiencing God.

Colossians 3:16 "Let the word of Christ dwell in you richly; teach and admonish one another in all wisdom; and with gratitude in your hearts sing psalms, hymns, and spiritual songs to God." (NRSV)

2. To learn about God. Church teaches us about God and more importantly how to apply God's truths to our lives. Maturing in Christ is becoming not only more knowledgeable, but also living a more applied life for Christ. If we are not learning, we are not growing. Remember, if you are only coasting, you are going downhill!

Acts 2:42 "They devoted themselves to the apostles' teaching and to the fellowship, to the breaking of bread and to prayer." (NIV)

3. Fellowship with God's people. Church should be a place where we can count on a group of like-minded Christ-followers to give us spiritual, emotional, social, and prayer support. A vibrant, healthy church is a large family. It is a family much larger than any family we can be a part of in any other manner—a caring, loving

family that encourages us as we encourage others.

Ephesians 2:10 "For we are God's workmanship, created in Christ Jesus to do good works, which God prepared in advance for us to do." (NIV)

4. To do good works for God. Your spiritual gifts can be discovered and matured at a local church. The church is an outlet to serve the body of Christ with the good works that God has prepared for us. The body only works well when all the parts are working together in harmony.

Part 4 – Measure Monthly

Lamentations 3:40 "Let us test and examine our ways, and return to the Lord." (NRSV)

2 Corinthians 13:5 "Examine yourselves to see whether you are living in the faith. Test yourselves. Do you not realize that Jesus Christ is in you?-unless, indeed, you fail to meet the test!" (NRSV)

Galatians 6:4 "All must test their own work; then that work, rather than their neighbor's work, will become a cause for pride." (NRSV)

Psalm 139:23 "Search me, O God, and know my heart; test me and know my thoughts." (NRSV)

Socrates once said, "An unexamined life is not worth living." I say an unexamined life is not biblical. An unexamined life is a life that is not being lived to its fullest potential, to the potential God intends for our life to be. It is a life not being lived out in abundance.

Jesus said in John 10:10, "The thief comes only to steal and kill and destroy. I came that they may have life, and have it abundantly." (NRSV)

What do I mean by measure monthly? At least once a month we should take time to measure our progress we are making in becoming more like Christ. We should measure our emotional balance, spiritual balance, and our physical balance. Sit down and ask yourself or even better sit down with an accountability partner and ask the tough questions. For your emotional balance, ask, "How am I handling the stresses in my life? How am I reacting to irritations? How am I handling the relationships in my life? Are my relationships with others becoming deeper and more meaningful or am I pushing people aside? Am I running so fast and so hard that emotionally I am numb or dead to the feelings I have and others have? Am I becoming more loving? More Christlike?"

For physical balance ask, "How are my eating habits?" You know the computer acronym, GIGO—Garbage In, Garbage Out? It applies to our bodies. "Am I getting regular exercise? Am I sleeping enough? Am I always worn down?"

For spiritual balance, I ask myself at least monthly, "Am I growing in Christ? Is my love for the Bible increasing? Is my love for Christ increasing? Is my love for people increasing? Is my heart growing bigger for the cause of Christ? Are my prayers more frequent and more heartfelt? Am I taking every opportunity to mature in Christ? How was my church attendance, my Bible study attendance, and my small group attendance last month?"

Finally abandon annually. At least once a year set aside a day to reflect on your life asking the same questions as monthly. Instead of making some New Year's resolutions make some New Life resolutions.

2 Corinthians 5:17 "Therefore, if anyone is in Christ, he is a new creation; the old has gone, the new has come." (NIV)

I have heard people say, I love God, I love people, I know my Bible, and I am going to coast on to the end from here. To which I reply, "You know if you are coasting, you have to be going downhill." You can't coast and grow. I don't want to get to the end and stand before God a stressed out, burned up, kicked around, shriveled-up heart, Christ-follower and say, "Well God, I coasted on to heaven." No, I want to stand before our Holy God with a great big grown heart and with a great big love for Christ. I want great love for people and I want to hear him say, "Well done My good and faithful servant, enter the Kingdom."

So, are you coasting or growing? I hope this series has caused you to stop long enough to at least examine the "gauges on your dashboard." I pray that something written in this series has triggered a change in your life. I pray that God uses these words, to touch you in a way that you can step back, look, and then move forward! All followers of Christ are going to heaven, no doubt about that. Why take the third -class seats, when you can go first-class? It's a great ride.

Chapter 7

Small Groups and Accountability

Part 1 – Four Relationships We All Need

1. We need models that inspire us.

   Jesus said in John 13:15, "I have given you an example to follow: do as I have done to you." (LB)

   Paul said in Philippians 3:17, "Dear brothers, pattern your lives after mine, and notice who else lives up to my example." (LB)

   Who are you following? Who are the models in your life?

2. We need mentors to advise us.

   Proverbs 19:20 "Get all the advice you can and be wise the rest of your life." (LB)

   Proverbs 15:22 "Plans go wrong with too few counselors;

many counselors bring success." (LB)

How to benefit from a mentor:

a: Ask questions - Proverbs 20:5 "Though good advice lies deep within a counselor's heart, the wise man will draw it out." (LB)
b: Accept feedback - Ecclesiastes 7:5 "It is better to be criticized by a wise man than to be praised by a fool!" (LB)

Proverbs 25:12 "It is a badge of honor to accept valid criticism." (LB)

3. We need partners that aid us.

Ecclesiastes 4:9-10 "Two can accomplish more than twice as much as one, for the results can be much better. If one falls, the other pulls him up; but if a man falls when he is alone, he's in trouble." (LB)

Romans 12:4-5 "Just as there are many parts to our bodies, so it is with Christ's body. We are all parts of it, and it takes every one of us to make it complete, for we each have different work to do. So we belong to each other, and each needs all the others." (LB)

4. We need friends that support us. True friends give the following:

Emotional Support – *Proverbs 17:17 "A true friend is always loyal, and a brother is born to help in time of need." (LB)*

Intellectual Support - *Proverbs 17:17 "Be with wise men and become wise. Be with evil men and become evil." (LB)*

Spiritual Support - *Hebrews 10:24 "In response to all he has done for us, let us outdo each other in being helpful and kind to each other and in doing good." (LB)*

2 Corinthians 6:15 "And what harmony can there be between Christ and the devil? How can a Christian be a partner with one who doesn't believe?" (LB)

1 Corinthians 15:33 "Don't be fooled by those who say such things. If you listen to them you will start acting like them." (LB)

And of course our most important relationship is that wonderful relationship with Jesus Christ.

Romans 5:11 "Now we rejoice in our wonderful new relationship with God-all because of what our Lord Jesus Christ has done in dying for our sins-making us friends of God." (LB)

Part 2 – Teaching and Sharing

Acts 2:46-47 "Every day they continued to meet together in the temple courts. They broke bread in their homes and ate together with glad and sincere hearts, praising God and enjoying the favor of all the people. And the Lord added to their number daily those who were being saved." (NIV)

Teaching and discipling a group of men is always a blessing for me. We meet every Tuesday morning for breakfast, prayer, praises, sharing of trials, and studying the Bible. We simply try to learn how to do life right and of course doing life right is doing it the way God wants us to do it. It is clear the early Christians did life right. They worshiped in the temples and met in small groups sharing and praising God. I am firmly convinced that solid, true, deep, life-changing growth in Christ occurs best in a small-group environment. For me the Sunday worship service is a celebration of our growth in Christ; it is the worship of our Holy God.

So now you may be saying, "Great David, thanks for sharing that, now I have to get to school, work, etc." Whoa... Hang on. What should we be doing? I urge you that if you are not in a small group, a care group, shepherding group, or whatever you want to call it, get into one. If you don't have one at your church, go to your pastor and get busy starting a group.

Now notice the last two sentences of the preceding verse, "Enjoying the favor of all the people. And the Lord added to their number daily those who were being saved." That's the goal folks, building the Kingdom. By living life right, these early Christian enjoyed the favor of all people, and the Kingdom is built one soul at a time. It's built one life at a time—touched by the life of someone else.

Part 3 – Accountability

Ecclesiastes 4:9-10 (NIV) "Two are better than one, because they have a good return for their work: If one falls down, his friend can help him up. But pity the man who falls and has no one to help him up!" Part two in this series talks about the value of being in a regular small group of believers to share and grow in Christ. Small groups, I think, are where growth occurs—while worship services are where we acknowledge God for whom He is, and celebrate our growth in Christ.

I want to take this a step further and talk about having an accountability partner. Being accountable to someone, gives us more incentive to be even more like Christ and to be more intimate with Christ. One reason we slip in our Christian walk is that we answer to no one. We don't intentionally start out the day and say, "Today I will fail in walking the talk." We have good plans. A person does not walk in a bar and say, "Today I think will become an alcoholic". No one wants to fail, no one intentionally misses the mark; a devoted Christ-follower does not intentionally fall into to the traps and snares that are placed before us in life.

Okay, let's get practical. How do I find a partner, and what is my accountability partner going to hold me accountable for? We must carefully choose our partner. Proverbs 13:20 (NIV) "He who walks with the wise grows wise, but a companion of fools suffers harm."

The primary issue which people I have talked with hold each other accountable for is the area of spiritual disciplines. Your partner can take a daily check-up on your Bible reading, prayer, quiet time, and other disciplines. In another words—holding you accountable for your relationship with God. Other areas are family, use of time and money, moral behavior, and personal struggles.

Building an accountability relationship with someone takes time—a lot of time. The most successful partners that I have seen have formed as an offshoot of a small group environment. Two people may connect in the group and then start meeting once a week on their own, to further develop their trust in each other, which leads to a true accountability relationship.

Next, let's talk more about what we should look for in an accountability partner, as well as discuss the relationship in more depth.

Part 4 – Choosing a Partner

Now let's look at what the Bible tells us about choosing an accountability partner.

James 5:16 "Therefore confess your sins to one another, and pray for one another, so that you may be healed. The prayer of the righteous is powerful and effective." (NRSV)

1 Thessalonians 5:11 "Therefore encourage one another and build up each other, as indeed you are doing." (NRSV)

Proverbs 17:17 "A friend loves you all the time, and a brother helps in time of trouble." (NCV)

First, let's look at what an accountability partner is not

1. This person is not a counselor to you, nor are you a counselor to them. A counselor is someone that you ask questions of and seek answers from. An accountability partner is someone that can ask us questions, and you are able to disclose the true answers. See the difference? In counseling, I go to someone and ask questions. With accountability, my partner comes to me and asks me the questions about my life. The partner can ask any question to help keep me on course.

2. An accountability partner is not a fellowship partner. You don't go to breakfast once a week and talk about the weather or the Chicago Bulls. You have to get beyond the mundane and surface-level conversations. You are allowing someone to see within you, to see past the smoke screens that we put up. It means getting past the Sunday morning conversation of, "How is life going?" and you saying, "Great, wonderful weather we are having," when actually you are struggling with sin, your kid is flunking in school, and your dog has quit speaking to you.

Is the picture of an accountability partner becoming clearer? This person must be someone on the same page or close to you spiritually. He or she also needs to be someone trustworthy and discreet. And the relationship needs to be on balance, an equal partnership. One partner does not dominate the relationship with his or her own problems. Now, of course, life challenges are not always equal. Some meetings or conversations with your partner will be one-sided; sometimes we need to just unload our burdens and that is great. But... over the course of the relationship, there is balance and equality in the sharing.

Finally, it plainly takes much prayer and time to find the ideal accountability partner. As I said earlier in this chapter, the ideal place to find a partner is in your small group. People will gravitate toward each other based on common interests and spiritual maturity.

Part 5 – Being Held Accountable

What do partners hold each other accountable for? My prayer is that some of you have taken the first steps to get involved in a small group, start a group, or develop a relationship with someone to be your accountability partner.

Now let's look at a suggested guideline for your weekly "Accountability Checkup" with your partner. However, I strongly believe we should never let a list of questions become a rigid syllabus for all accountability meetings. Let the Holy Spirit guide and direct the meetings.

"The kisses of an enemy may be profuse, but faithful are the

wounds of a friend" Proverbs 27:6 (NIV)

This list comes from Patrick Morely's book, *Getting to know the Man in the Mirror*, published by Thomas Nelson Publishers.

Questions to start off your meeting.
How has God blessed you this week? (What went right?)
What problem has consumed your thoughts this week? (What went wrong?)
Spiritual Life
Have you read God's Word daily? (How long? Why not? Will you next week?)
Describe your prayers (for you, others, praise, confession, gratitude)
How is your relationship with Christ changing?
How have you been tempted this week? How did you respond?
Do you have any unconfessed sin in your life?
Are you walking in the Spirit?
Did you worship in church this week? (Was your faith in Jesus strengthened? Was He honored?)
Have you shared your faith? In what ways? How can you improve?
Home Life
How is it going with your spouse? (attitudes, time, irritations, disappointments, progress, their relationship with Christ)
How is it going with the kids? (quantity and quality of time, values and beliefs, education, spiritual welfare and warfare)
How are your finances going? (debts, sharing, saving, stewardship)

Work Life
How are things going on the job? (career progress, relationships, temptations, workload, stress, problems, working too much)
Critical Concerns
Do you feel you are in the center of God's will? Do you sense His peace?
What are you wrestling with in your thought life?
What have you done for someone else this week? (helping the poor, offering encouragement, providing service)
Are your priorities in the right order?

Is your moral and ethical behavior what it should be?
How are you doing in your personal high-risk area?
Are the "visible" you and the "real" you consistent in this relationship?

Close with Prayer.

That's it. I pray all of you can develop an accountability relationship.

Chapter 8

Twelve Steps for Christian Living

Part 1 – Powerless

Romans 7:18 "I know I am rotten through and through, so far as my old sinful nature is concerned. No matter which way I turn, I can't make myself do right. I want to, but I can't." (NLT)

I want you to take a journey with me along a path of recovery. I am going to "borrow" liberally from the original Twelve Steps program designed in the 1930's by Bill Wilson for recovering alcoholics. I have tweaked the steps to help us become more Christlike. I am not an expert on these steps. The more I learn about them, the more I find they can apply to all of us. These tools help us understand ourselves and manage our lives through God's help. The Twelve Steps is a spiritual program, and I pray that through this series, we can be closer to our God who is greater than us and is still in control. Come now; let's go on this journey and see where God takes us.

Step 1 – We admitted we were powerless over our sinful nature—that our lives had become unmanageable.

Galatians 5:19-21a "When you follow the desires of your sinful nature, your lives will produce these evil results: sexual immorality, impure thoughts, eagerness for lustful pleasure, idolatry, participation in demonic activities, hostility, quarreling, jealousy, outbursts of anger, selfish ambition, divisions, the feeling that everyone is wrong except those in your own little group, envy, drunkenness, wild parties, and other kinds of sin." (NLT)

We are all born with this sinful nature. The sin of Adam is imputed to all his descendants; therefore we are all in need of recovery. Without God managing our lives, we cannot experience life to the fullest. Step one is a difficult step, because it is both counterintuitive and countercultural. Our American way is that we can do life how we want to do life. We don't need help from anyone, and especially not from an unseen God. Maybe you are like me and play the part of the "Lone Ranger," falsely believing that you control everything around you.

But on our own, we are powerless over our sinful nature, and we need a catalyst to help us overcome this built-in desire to sin. That change agent, of course, is Christ. As Paul writes in the passage above, when we follow our sinful nature, our lives become unmanageable. Perhaps work is your addiction, and your home life has become unmanageable. The Christian way of living seeks a life like Christ—a balanced life submitted to God's will.

Romans 3:10, 23 "As the Scriptures say, 'No one is good-not even one.' For all have sinned; all fall short of God's glorious standard." (NLT)

The Bible is clear that none of us can do life on our own, and we cannot live an eternity with God, without admitting to ourselves and to God that we need a Savior. Have you at least taken that first step? If not, I will be glad to help you. Apart from Christ our Savior, these 12 Steps are not powerful from a Christian perspective. We

Christians need the power of God living within us, to overcome our sinful nature. When we accept Christ as our Savior, He takes house in us through the Holy Sprit, to help us live manageable lives.

But most of you have probably have already accepted Christ. Now is the time for us to reflect, to go countercultural, and to realize that we are powerless over something or some areas in our lives. And here is the important part: Our lives have become unmanageable.

Part 2 – Belief

2 Corinthians 12:8-9 "Three different times, I begged the Lord to take it away. Each time he said, My gracious favor is all you need. My power works best in your weakness. So now I am glad to boast about my weaknesses, so the power of Christ may work through me." (NLT)

Step 2 – We come to believe that God, a Power greater than ourselves, can restore us to sanity.

In Step one, we admit that we are powerless over our sinful natures and that our lives are unmanageable. Step two introduces us to the real power than can restore our broken and sinful lives to sanity. The American Heritage Dictionary defines sanity as, "the quality or condition of being sane; soundness of mind. Soundness of judgment or reason." In other words a sane person is a good decision maker. As Christians, we want to make decisions that honor God. A sane person does not hang around temptations that he cannot control. A sane person does not rationalize away all of his faults. A sane person comes to believe in God and His power.

If we don't have the power that is greater than ourselves, how do we receive it? What is it? Who is it? Paul cries out in the following passage, asking this Power to save him from his unsound judgment or his insanity.

Romans 7:24-25 "Oh, what a miserable person I am! Who will free me from this life that is dominated by sin? Thank God! The answer is in Jesus Christ our Lord. So you see how it is: In my mind, I want to obey God's law, but because of my sinful nature, I am a slave to sin." (NLT)

Paul was struggling with his self-centered, sinful nature. He was miserable. Frustrated and weary, we often cry out, "I am sick and tired of being sick and tired!" I believe this is what Paul is finally saying in his surrendering attitude toward God. We receive His power by accepting His son Christ as our Savior. It is a gift for the asking.

Revelation 3:20 "Look! Here I stand at the door and knock. If you hear me calling and open the door, I will come in, and we will share a meal as friends." (NLT)

The path of restoration and recovery is not an easy path. The road has dips, bumps, plateaus, and high points—and it never ends. Paul finds the answer, just as we can, in Jesus. We have to come to believe that Christ can restore us. This restoration makes us right with God. Restoration makes something old new. This rightness with God gives us the power, through his Holy Spirit, to be sane and have good judgment.

Romans 8:1-4 "So now there is no condemnation for those who belong to Christ Jesus. For the power of the life-giving Spirit has freed you, through Christ Jesus, from the power of sin that leads to death. The Law of Moses could not save us, because of our sinful nature. But God put into effect a different plan to save us. He sent his own Son in a human body like ours, except that ours are sinful. God destroyed sin's control over us by giving his Son as a sacrifice for our sins. He did this so that the requirement of the law would be fully accomplished for us who no longer follow our sinful nature but instead follow the Spirit." (NLT)

Are you ready to take the second step? Are you ready to surrender to God by believing that you are not the center of the universe? You are not all-powerful. You are not all-knowing. You are not the answer. You are not the restoring power. And you are not in control of your restoration and sanity? Sound judgments do not come to us apart from the God that created us.

Part 3 – Decision Time

Step 3 – We make a decision to turn our lives over to the care and will of God.

Matthew 11:28-30 "Then Jesus said, 'Come to me, all of you who are weary and carry heavy burdens, and I will give you rest. Take my yoke upon you. Let me teach you, because I am humble and gentle, and you will find rest for your souls. For my yoke fits perfectly, and the burden I give you is light.'" (NLT)

Eugene Peterson beautifully paraphrases this passage in The Message: "Are you tired? Worn out? Burned-out on religion? Come to me. Get away with me and you'll recover your life. I'll show you how to take a real rest. Walk with me and work with me—watch how I do it. Learn the unforced rhythms of grace. I won't lay anything heavy or ill-fitting on you. Keep company with me and you'll learn to live freely and lightly."

In Step one, we admitted that we are powerless over our sinful nature. In Step two, we came to believe that God, through his Son Jesus, could restore us to sane living. It is one thing to believe Steps one and two are true, but another to carry out this biblical plan. Step three brings us to that implementation, to a decision time. Are we going to turn our lives and wills over to the care of God? Steps one and two are the basis for our decision. The Bible must have authority in our lives for us to have this basis. The steps are not the foundation for our decision in Step three, but rather tools to give us the realization that we must make a decision.

Let me explain with this story. There was a large pasture filled with people. The pasture had a wooden fence running down the middle. Jesus and the Evil One were watching the people milling around. Jesus calls out to the people: "All of you that want to follow me, go to the right side of the fence." After a while, Jesus and His followers walked away. One person was left standing on top of the fence. The Evil One said to him, "Come with me now." The man replied, "But I am on the fence." The Evil One answered, "I own the fence; come now."

Proverbs 16:3 "Commit your work to the Lord, and then your plans will succeed." (NLT)

If you are on the fence, it is time to make a choice. It is time to acquire the power that is greater than us. It is time to receive the One who can turn our broken, weary, insane, and unmanageable lives into the lives that He has planned for us.

1 John 4:15-16 "All who proclaim that Jesus is the Son of God have God living in them, and they live in God. We know how much God loves us, and we have put our trust in him." (NLT)

Are you ready to take Step three? Are you ready for Christ to be the basis for your decision? Are you ready to turn all parts of your life and will over to His care? Are you ready to start really living? If you have committed to change your life and turn it over to God, can people around you see the change? For some of us, it is time to move the head knowledge to our heart and then on to our feet. It is time to make your changed life obvious to those around you.

I asked a horse trainer friend of mine recently about another trainer. In his dry wit, he replied, "Well, if horse training were a crime, it would be a crime to hang him." In other words, there was no evidence of him being a true horse trainer. Is there evidence in your life that you have decided to grow? If you accepted Christ before, maybe it is time to recommit your life and will to Him.

Romans 10:9 "For if you confess with your mouth that Jesus is Lord and believe in your heart that God raised him from the dead, you will be saved." (NLT)

Come on and get off the fence. This simple prayer will take you to the right side of the pasture.

Jesus, I am a sinner in need of a Savior and a manager of my life, will, and eternity. I believe in You. I believe that You died and rose again so I may live. Come into my heart today and take control of my life. By your authority I pray, Amen.

Part 4 – Inventory Time

Step 4 – We made a searching and fearless moral inventory of ourselves.

Psalm 139:23-24 (NIV)"Search me, O God, and know my heart; test me and know my anxious thoughts. Point out anything in me that offends you, and lead me along the path of everlasting life."

Steps one through three are preparatory steps for Step four. Here is a brief summary of the first three steps. Step one: We recognized that we are powerless over our sinful nature and that our lives have become unmanageable on our own. In Step two, we came to believe the God who created us could restore us to sane living. Step three: We simply decided to turn our lives and will over to the care of God.

For me, and I would think most Christians, we go through life doing the Steps one, two, three; one, two, three—and on we waltz, dancing through life to our own tune never making it to the fourth step. We realize there is a problem, cry out to God for help, and then make ourselves believe we given our lives and will over to God. As time passes and the problem subsides, we fall back into our self-centered ways. No need for God right now, everything is going great! Or we do the famous cafeteria-style of Step three: Here, God, you can have this, that, and a helping of this, but you can't touch these parts of my life.

Step three can be a spiritual plateau on which we become stuck. We settle in on this comfort zone. Like water in a puddle, we become stale, stagnant, and stoic Christians—or worse, we slip off the plateau to where we once were. Plateaus can be and should be wonderful events in our lives. They are places to rest, catch our breath, and think about the future, but they are not a place to stop forever.

Step four begins the carrying out our decision to turn our lives and will over to God. This is a lifelong step. We will grow, plateau, and then grow some more, all in God's time and His will.

Step Four can be scary for most of us. The Psalmist's prayer above is a frightening prayer. I urge you to pray this prayer when doing Step four. This does not need to be a scary step; rather, it can be an exciting step to help us out of our bondage of rationalization and delusional, sinful living. This step simply identifies the faults that have separated us from God.

1 John 1:8-10 (NLT) "If we say we have no sin, we are only fooling ourselves and refusing to accept the truth. But if we confess our sins to him, he is faithful and just to forgive us and to cleanse us from every wrong. If we claim we have not sinned, we are calling God a liar and showing that his word has no place in our hearts." This Bible passage is one of my favorites. It takes us out of a delusional state of mind. I define delusional here as "making our own reality". It is not real that none of us are without faults. It is not real that we are perfect. It is, however, real that we can become developing followers of Christ. We can live a life that moves along a path of growth—not of perfection but rather progression.

At this point in the 12 Step program, an accountability partner, mentor, or as they say in A.A. a sponsor, is an invaluable tool. A mentor is someone that has walked the path before you. He or she has seen the highs and the lows, reached the plateaus and moved on. He understands the process, and in turn will help you.

Obviously I love to write. I write most of my prayers to God. Step four should be a written inventory of what is keeping you from becoming more like Christ. We simply write the nature of our character defects. Do not rush this step. Take all the time you need.

While there is not a right or wrong way to being this process, here is an outline that will help you begin. This list is not original. It comes from talking to people I know that are in 12 Step Recovery programs such as Alcoholic Anonymous.

1. Begin by writing down your resentments. Resentment is defined as "indignation or ill will felt because of real or imagined grievance." A synonym is anger. What or who are you resentful toward? What causes this anger? What effect is it having on your life and your relationship to God? What was your role in causing this behavior?

2. Fears. What do you fear? What causes this fear? What effect

is this having on your life and your closeness to God?

3. Sexuality Instincts. This includes how you relate to people of the opposite sex. Not just sexual encounters. What is your behavior and attitude about this? How does it affect your life and relationship with God?

4. Financial security. What are your behaviors and attitudes toward money and managing your finances? What is causing these attitudes? What are the effects on your life and your relationship with God?

5. Emotional security. Again, what behavior and attitudes are causing you emotional problems? Emotional insecurity can lead to depression, fear, worry, self-pity and anger. What relationships are causing me emotional insecurity?

6. Social instincts. Do you have any social connections that cause you pain? Do you behave in an irrational way, to make yourself out to be someone that you are not, due to your social insecurity?

I am sure there are more items to list. In short, what behavior and attitudes are causing you separation from God? What are you doing that is harmful to others? What are you doing that is harmful to you?

At the end of this inventory, please write the positive characteristics of yourself. There is good in everyone. Don't use this list to beat yourself up. Rather, use it as a benchmark, a starting point from which to grow. Your best effort to do a complete and honest inventory shows your willingness to turn your life and will over to God.

Part 5 – Confession Time

Step 5 – We admitted to God, to ourselves, and to another human being the exact nature of our wrongs.

I hope you are still with me on this journey through the Twelve Steps. In Step four we began the process of carrying out our decision to turn our lives and will over to God. This is a lifelong process. We will grow, plateau, and then grow some more, all in God's time and His will. We wrote down all the stumbling blocks in our lives that keep us from a right relationship with God.

Step five is a confessional step. This confession helps to relieve us of the burdens, bindings, and baggage we uncovered in Step four. To do this step, we must have a trusted person who will hear and listen to our written personal inventory from Step four. Why confess to another person, you ask? Can't I just confess to God? He knows all my wrongs. Well, I can't trust this mental playground called my mind, to just myself. I may secretly confess some wrongs to God. Without another person, I am prone to beat myself up over and over again for what my mind and the evil one will lead me to believe is an unforgiving and unforgotten sin.

James 5:16 "Confess your sins to each other and pray for each other so that you may be healed. The earnest prayer of a righteous person has great power and wonderful results." (NLT)

Proverbs 28:13 "People who cover over their sins will not prosper. But if they confess and forsake them, they will receive mercy." (NLT)

The person with whom we share our flaws is not the object of our confession; God is and we are. And He does want to hear our confessions. But we need a mentor to keep us on track and be nonjudgmental. This mentor must be a trusted, seasoned, and spiritually mature person. And when we wallow again and again in our past foul-ups, our mentors can remind us that we confessed them and that we have been forgiven. Step five is not only a step of confession; it is also a step toward healing.

The 5th Step also helps break the isolation we feel from others, not just God. When we are vulnerable and honest, deeply honest, with another human being, somehow that experience makes us less fearful to be of use to others. Farther along in the Steps, we will plow through the wreckage, weakness, worries, and wrongs that keep us apart from God. Our goal is rightness with God, and in turn, we live the way God intended—lives not bound by past resentments and fears.

We are only as sick as our secrets. When we admit our wrongs to another person, we no longer fear our secrets, nor are we immobilized by them. We are now ready to make more progress in our journey to becoming more like Christ, by turning our lives and will over to the care of God.

Jesus states in Luke 12:2-3 "The time is coming when everything will be revealed; all that is secret will be made public." (NLT)

Whatever you have said in the dark will be heard in the light, and what you have whispered behind closed doors will be shouted from the housetops for all to hear!

Friends, the time has come. The time has come to quit hiding behind a false façade, a mask that we put in front of our true self. The time has come to break through the prison that we place ourselves in by hiding and quivering in fear.

Step 6 – Contemplation

Step 6 – We are entirely ready to have God remove all these defects of character.

Isaiah 1:19 "If you will only obey me and let me help you, then you will have plenty to eat." (NLT)

2 Timothy 2:15 "Work hard so God can approve you. Be a good worker, one who does not need to be ashamed and who correctly explains the word of truth." (NLT)

In Step four, we made a fearless, searching inventory of ourselves. In Step five, we had a confession time to another person and to God. Step six sounds simple, but it is difficult and important. It is time to get our hearts ready to allow God to work more in our lives. Step six is a contemplative step. It asks us to look back to see if we've been holding on to some secret or reservation, but mostly it is a step that takes a good, hard look at our faith.

We have come to the point where we will see if we are absolutely and totally willing to have God remove our past sinful ways. Do we have enough faith in God to let Him soften our hearts? Are we willing to accept His mercies, grace, love, and peace? Do we trust Him with our entire lives?

Just as when we were doing our personal inventory in Step four, we need to avoid the trap of being willing to give only certain parts of our lives over to God. We cannot make our lives into cafeteria lines, telling God, "Well you may have only two vegetables and one meat—and no desserts!"

Step six asks, "Do we have enough faith, unreserved faith, to trust the Lord will fill, with His goodness and love, the void left when we are willing to set aside our sinful natures?" Steps four and five have allowed me to get honest about how lustful thoughts separate me from God and those around me. Step six asks me if I honestly have the faith to give those lustful thoughts to God, while believing the Lord's goodness and grace will fill whatever panicked spiritual hole the lustful thoughts were soothing. Am I willing to let go of my way of taking care of my selfish needs, and to step aside and have God take care of my needs, as well as decide what those needs are?

This seemingly simple step is a direct question of our faith in God to handle our lives. The following verse best describes this:

1 John 5:4-5 "For every child of God defeats this evil world by trusting Christ to give the victory. And the ones who win this battle against the world are the ones who believe that Jesus is the Son of God." (NLT)

Everyday I hear God asking me, "David, do you really trust me? Do you really have faith in me?"

Do you?

Step 7 – Removal

Step 7 – We humbly asked Him to remove our shortcomings.

James 4:10 "Humble yourselves in the sight of the Lord, and he shall lift you up." (KJV)

James 4:10 "When you bow down before the Lord and admit your dependence on him, he will lift you up and give you honor." (NLT)

Just what does it mean to be humble? Humility is defined as "marked by meekness or modesty in behavior, attitude, or spirit; not arrogant or prideful. It is showing deferential or submissive respect." Being humble is the opposite of being self-centered. It's time for us to stop playing God and let God do His work in our lives. It is time to humbly submit our entire beings to Him.

The key to Step seven is having the humility and faith to turn all of ourselves over to God, to ask Him to remove all of our shortcomings. I want to say to God, "Okay you take care of these big sins and flaws, and I will take the little ones." Or something like, "Okay God, thanks for getting me out of that jam; now I will take it from here." Some of us say, "God can have me on Sunday morning, but come Monday, all bets are off!" Maybe you have decided to be a dedicated husband, but your actions at work are off-limits to God. The question we need to ask of ourselves: "Is God the Lord of our entire life or just part?"

Jeremiah 18:6b "As the clay is in the potter's hand, so are you in my hand." (NLT)

In Step six, we talked about having real faith. Do we have the faith to trust God entirely? Step seven is the practical application of that faith. Sure, we might buy what the Lord Jesus Christ offers us through his sacrifice, the forgiveness of sin and everlasting life—but are we willing to make practical, concrete applications of that faith for individual parts of our sinful nature?

Step seven is a leap of faith and an acknowledgment that we want and welcome God's design for who and what He wants us to be. We entrust all of ourselves into God care, so He can mold, shape, and influence us—so we may better do His will and work. He is the potter; we are the clay. He is Lord of all.

For God to remove defects from our lives, we have to give our lives to Him and turn away from the defect. Repentance is simply "turning away." It is going in one direction and then taking a 180-degree turn in the other direction. Having the faith and the humility to submit our lives to God is not enough. God will do His part, but we still need to do our part. If we want change, we have to make changes in our lives. We can't ask God to keep us from being lustful, but then keep hanging out at the "gentleman's club." God can guide us and direct us, but He loves us so much that he still allows us to have the free will to do as we please.

Okay, I hear some of you out there, "but David I can't go to God with this. You don't know how bad I have been!" As we say here in the South, "You ain't telling me nothing I don't know." God knows everything about you. But just as a loving parent wants his child to ask for help and forgiveness in times of need, so does God. God is not too busy, not too big, not too powerful, and not too burdened to help you. Just ask.

The writer of Hebrews sums up Step seven in this way:

Hebrews 4:14-16 "That is why we have a great High Priest who has gone to heaven, Jesus the Son of God. Let us cling to him and never stop trusting him. This High Priest of ours understands our weaknesses, for he faced all the same temptations we do, yet he did not sin. So let us come boldly to the throne of our gracious God. There we will receive his mercy, and we will find grace to help us when we need it." (NLT)

Step seven is simply transferring the control of our lives over to God. It is putting ourselves in God's hand as unformed clay, asking Him to shape us and mold us into the person that He intended for us to become. It is letting God decide which defects are standing in our way of being not only who He wants us to be, but also what keeps us from being close to Him and those around us.

Ready to stop trying to play God? Ready to stop banging your head against the wall while trying to fix yourself? Join me in a prayer that I have adapted from AA's "Big Book." This prayer is our first move toward the freedom of turning our lives completely over to God.

All-powerful God, I am now willing for you to have all of me, both good and bad. I pray that you now remove from me every single defect of character that stands in the way of my usefulness to you and those around me. Give me your strength to turn away from the faults that I have, and to turn toward You. You are the potter and I am the clay. Hold me, mold me and recreate me into what You want. In your Son's name I pray, Amen.

Part 8 – Making Amends

Step 8 – Make a list of all people we have harmed and become willing to make amends to them all.

Matthew 4:3-5 "And why worry about a speck in your friend's eye when you have a log in your own? How can you think of saying, Let me help you get rid of that speck in your eye, when you can't see past the log in your own eye? Hypocrite! First get rid of the log from your own eye; then perhaps you will see well enough to deal with the speck in your friend's eye." (NLT)

In Step seven, we looked inward at ourselves and asked God to humbly remove our shortcomings. In Step eight, we are going to look outward at those we have harmed and become willing to make amends. Again this is a step of preparation. We become willing to love others as ourselves.

Step eight is a preparatory step, much like Step four. We need to be able to take a close, hard, and honest look at our actions and ourselves. This needs to be done without the great denial part of us telling ourselves that we are perfect and everyone else is at fault. We need to avoid self-justification of our actions. We need to stop saying, "Lord, why is everyone against me? Why can't people see this my way? Why can't people be like me?" Instead, we need to say, "Lord, help me see how my sinful nature has harmed others, and Lord, make me willing and humble enough to make amends to them all."

This is a step that looks at our personal relationships with others and how those damaged relationships prevent us from having a closer relationship with God. Our God is a God that loves relationships. He loves relationships with us and we have good solid relationship with others. Broken relationships usually harbor pain, guilt, resentment, and other relationship blocking emotions inside us. These painful emotions must be cleaned out of our dark moldy basements of our past.

So, how do I start with Step eight? Just as with Step four, a written list of all those people you have harmed is the best way to start. Ask yourself: "Who have I harmed? How did I harm them? What was the result of my action toward them?" Do you see a pattern of behavior that is damaging to those around you? Make your list and pray, "Lord, make me willing to be forgiving of myself, my actions, and able to try to make amends."

Mark 11:22 (NLT) "But when you are praying, first forgive anyone you are holding a grudge against, so that your Father in heaven will forgive your sins, too."

1 Peter 4:8 (NLT) "Most important of all, continue to show deep love for each other, for love covers a multitude of sins."

For me, I do not believe Step eight can be done without a mentor, sponsor, or trusted Christian friend looking over your list to give you an unbiased opinion of it. This is essential before moving on to Step nine. In addition, we must be healthy spiritually to do Step eight. These 12 Steps are lifelong. Step eight comes down the road of maturity gained from Steps 1-7. There is no need to rush through this program. Walk slowly, tread lightly, honoring God along the way. Then He, in turn, will honor your actions.

Hebrews 12:14 "Make every effort to live in peace with all men and to be holy; without holiness no one will see the Lord." (NIV)

Part 9 – Make Amends

Step 9 – Make direct amends to such people wherever possible, except when to do so would injure them or others.

Matthew 5:23-24 (The Message) This is how I want you to conduct yourself in these matters. If you enter your place of worship and, about to make an offering, you suddenly remember a grudge a friend has against you, abandon your offering, leave immediately, go to this friend and make things right. Then and only then, come back and work things out with God.

In Step Eight, we made a list of all the people we have harmed and asked God to make us willing to make amends with them. Step Eight prepares us for Step Nine. I want to remind all of you, at this point, that these steps cannot be taken out of order. Each step builds upon the previous one. Just reading Step Nine terrifies me to the point of saying, "well, I am finished with these steps." Hang in here with me, and remember we are on a journey. It's a long trip, not a short jaunt to the corner store.

The above passage is the only one that I can find where God tell us to leave worship **before** giving our offering. Making amends with others must be very important to God. I believe the passage is implying that if we have problems with others, then we will have problems with our relationship with God. If I am full of guilt from my past, or bundled up in a cocoon of anger against someone, then I have walls between God and myself.

Step Nine must be taken with the utmost care, wisdom, prudence and prayerful guidance of timing and words. It is a must, at this point, to have a trusted friend, a seasoned Christian — and even better — a person that has been through Step Nine himself or herself. This accountability partner or sponsor will hopefully prevent you from making some critical mistakes, and will help you make these direct amends in the most appropriate way, which will injure neither the person you are seeking to make amends with nor others.

Don't expect the other person to accept your offer of making the amends. Some will accept your offer and embrace you with compassion and forgiveness; others will reject you and send you away. Be prepared to accept both forgiveness and rejection. Take them both with humility. **Give them both to God.**

If the person does forgive you, handle with care! Forgiveness, for some of us, is just as hard to accept as rejection.

You will also be very wise to avoid a "holier-than-thou" attitude toward others. All God asks us to do is to attempt to be reconciled with others. Then we must let go and turn the situation over to God.

The most obvious people on your list are family members. Go to them first, and ask their forgiveness for the wrongs you have committed against them. Tell them you are working on your life by turning your will over to God. The key is to go slowly. Do not overwhelm others; just let them know you are working on yourself.

We never want to attempt to make amends when it will harm or injure another person. Sexual sins are the most frequent sin in which amends cannot practically be made. You may feel guilty about having an affair with another man's wife, but it would most likely destroy their marriage if you went to his wife or him, asking for forgiveness. Old flames are probably not to be tracked down, even if there's no harm to be done to the other person. With the impulse to make amends to old flames, it is imperative to check one's motive. Never make amends at someone else's expense. Never.

What about people that we can no longer be in contact with? Perhaps the person has died or moved away. I have written many letters that wound up in my paper shredder. But the process of writing the letter had a great healing effect. Writing out your confession and asking forgiveness brings you from the point of denial about your problem, to the realization that you were the problem or at least a part of the problem.

Make amends with yourself. Honestly try to forgive yourself for the harm you have caused to yourself. Often our sin disease harms us more than others. Be willing to forgive yourself, to accept your forgiveness and to accept the forgiveness that God will give you.

Is Step Nine easy? No way. I will emphasize, once again, the importance of handling Step Nine with the utmost prudence.

John 3:11 (NLT) This is the message we have heard from the beginning: We should love one another.

Part 10 – Continuation

Step 10 – Continue to take personal inventory, and when we are wrong, promptly admit it.

Mark 14:38 "Keep alert and pray. Otherwise temptation will overpower you. For though the spirit is willing enough, the body is weak." (NLT)

Luke 9:23 "Then he said to the crowd, "If any of you wants to be my follower, you must put aside your selfish ambition, shoulder your cross daily, and follow me." (NLT)

The first nine steps are major repairs. Steps 10-12 are maintenance steps. The first nine steps are akin to serious surgery on our lives. Step ten is daily maintenance of our lives.

On the surface, Step ten appears to be an easy step that can be skimmed over. But it's not! Taking a daily inventory of our lives is crucial to our recovery from our sinful nature. Step ten is difficult to carry out, because of the fast-paced, hectic lifestyles most of us live. It is easy—in the heat of the battle—to toss aside the foundation and the truths that Christ has laid down for us to live by.

Living our new lives in Christ is a moment-by-moment goal. In every situation we face, ideally we would stop and think, "How can I best react to this as Christ would?" For example, say that your co-worker, classmate, or friend has told another person an untrue story about you. When you find out, your mind and heart should shift toward the first three steps. Think: First, I am powerless over what this person has done. Secondly, if I react in my way, then I will display my insanity. And thirdly, I should turn this over to God and let Him guide my reaction.

Step Ten helps us preserve balance in our lives. It keeps us dependent on God and not ourselves. We recognize that God alone is in control, and we are simply trying our best to follow His will in every situation that we face. Before the major surgery of Steps 1-9, we may have turned to drugs, rage, or other unacceptable behavior that harmed ourselves and those around us. Step ten is a stop sign advising us to "Stop and think!"

We learn from our mistakes. Sometimes at the end of the day, we may need to hit the rewind button and carefully analyze a situation that occurred during the day—and how we handled that situation. When someone angered us, how did we respond? Were we wrong? Were we right? Did we follow God's will? Did we stop and realize that God is in control? Did we turn the situation over to God, or did we try to be in control of the event?

As always, this does not mean beating ourselves up daily. Think of the positive reactions you had as well. Ask yourself, "What did I do right today? How have I grown today? Am I a little more like Christ at the end of today, than I was at the beginning?"

Part 11 – Prayer

Step 11 – Seek through prayer and meditation to improve our conscious contact with God as revealed in the Bible, praying only for knowledge of His will for us and the power to carry that out.

James 4:8a "Draw close to God, and God will draw close to you." (NLT)

Step Eleven is an "action" step. It is asking us to do two disciplines—to pray and to meditate. Now when I first read this step, I was concerned about praying only for the knowledge of His will. But as I meditated (no pun intended) on this step, it began to come alive for me.

One of the main goals of the Twelve Steps is to move us away from playing God—and instead allowing God to be God in our lives. We do this by becoming aware of walls between us and God in the first nine steps. Now in Step eleven, we are going to draw closer to God through prayer and meditation.

For the past three years, I have helped out a man who has been mostly homeless and without a job. I prayed and prayed for "Kenny." God get him a job, God do this, God do that. Now here is the radical truth for me which I finally realized: When God did not answer my prayers about Kenny as I wanted Him to, I then "played

God." I took matters into my own hands. He would come by the office needing money, and I would give it to him. But about six months ago, I decided that perhaps it was not my place to just keep giving Kenny money. His promises to me of a job never panned out.

So, I simply said, "God, you take him." Just two days ago, Kenny called me to tell me that he finally got a job! Well, I was hampering God's will by playing God. As long as I gave Kenny money, he did not need to look hard for a job. In the term I hear often from members of Alcoholics Anonymous, I was "enabling" Kenny to not work. Once I got out of God's way, He could work.

I believe that often when prayers are not answered to our liking or in our time frame, we answer them ourselves. This step, in telling us to pray only for the knowledge of God's will, removes us out of the danger zone of wanting to push God aside. It puts us in the role that we need to live out—the role of God's children, rather than God Himself.

Is it okay to pray for people and other matters? Of course it is okay! Jesus prayed, in the verse below, for the suffering of the cross to be removed from Him. But notice He states, "Your will, not mine."

Luke 22:42 "Father, if you are willing, please take this cup of suffering away from me. Yet I want your will, not mine." (NLT)

So, if we take hold of Step twelve and believe prayer and meditation are important, here are four reasons to pray.

The first and most obvious reason to pray is God's command that we do so. Prayer is an act of obedience, on our part, toward God.

Matthew 26:41 "Watch and pray so that you will not fall into temptation. The spirit is willing, but the body is weak." (NIV)

Matthew 6:6 "But when you pray, go into your room, close the door and pray to your Father, who is unseen. Then your Father, who sees what is done in secret, will reward you." (NIV)

Notice Jesus did not say, "If you pray" or "When you feel like praying." He said, "When you pray." He expects us to pray.

Secondly, God knows everything, yet His general will allows for flexibility in our involvement in carrying out His work. For example, while He may have chosen me to play a role in leading someone to Christ, He allows me to make the choice of accepting or turning down the opportunity. If I choose not to, then I lose the blessing of being a part of God's plan, but this person will still be saved. Someone else will be part of the plan, in my place. God wants us to be participants in His plans, not just observers.

Ephesians 1:3-5 "How we praise God, the Father of our Lord Jesus Christ, who has blessed us with every blessing in heaven because we belong to Christ." (LB)

Long ago, even before He made the world, God chose us to be His own, through what Christ would do for us. He decided then, to make us holy in His eyes, without a single fault—we who stand before Him covered with His love. His unchanging plan has always been to adopt us into His own family, by sending Jesus Christ to die for us. And He did this because He wanted to! Even before the beginning of time, God started dealing with us. What an awesome fact to grasp! He has a plan for His children, and we can be a part of it by our prayers.

Thirdly, prayer is an act of submission, on our part, to God. We are not submissive by nature. Many men that I speak with have trouble getting down on their knees and praying to God, because they don't feel in control, or somehow believe it is unmanly. But submission to God is a key to the Christian life and fulfilling His perfect plans for us.

Finally, prayer is about our communion and fellowship with God. Through prayer, we grow closer to Him and become more concerned about seeking His will, than about receiving our answers.

1 John 1:3-4 "We proclaim to you what we have seen and heard, so you also may have fellowship with us. And our fellowship is with the Father and with his Son, Jesus Christ. We write this to make our joy complete." (NIV)

Acts 2:42 "They devoted themselves to the apostles' teaching and to the fellowship, to break bread and to prayer." (NIV)

The second part of Step eleven is to meditate. Praying is us talking to God, while meditation is us trying to listen to God. We simply ask God for His will; then we are to be quiet, to be still, and to listen. This is a tough discipline that takes a great amount of time to fully conquer the distractions in our lives and to be still.

I recommend reading a passage in the Bible or a short devotional, and then praying to God for the meaning of this for your life and how it is in His will. There are real misunderstandings about meditation. We too often think we must produce something during meditation, which is not necessarily so. Meditation is the time we take to rest our heads and hearts in quietness, so that during the rest of the day we are more efficient and effective in hearing the Lord and doing His will. God does not have to "speak" to us during meditation for meditation to be effective. Rest. That's the key.

Now, don't beat yourself up, and don't go and try to pray and meditate for an hour, the first time. Start with shorter time frames—five minutes—and then work up to more time. I find that writing my prayers keeps me from being distracted. I also have found that having a quiet place, and praying at the same time each day, keeps me in touch with God. Whatever works for you, then do it.

Part Twelve – An Awakening

Step Twelve – Having had a spiritual awakening as a result of these steps, we tried to carry this message to others, and practice these principles in all our affairs.

1 Timothy 1:12-14 (NLT) How thankful I am to Christ Jesus our Lord, for considering me trustworthy and appointing me to serve him, even though I used to scoff at the name of Christ. I hunted down his people, harming them in every way I could. But God had mercy on me, because I did it in ignorance and unbelief. Oh, how kind and gracious the Lord was! He filled me completely with faith and the love of Christ Jesus.

This is a true saying, and everyone should believe it: Christ Jesus came into the world to save sinners and I was the worst of them all. But that is why God had mercy on me, so that Christ Jesus could use me as a prime example of his great patience with even the worst sinners. Then others will realize that they, too, can believe in him and receive eternal life.

Matthew 28:19-20 (NLT) Therefore, go and make disciples of all the nations, baptizing them in the name of the Father and the Son and the Holy Spirit. Teach these new disciples to obey all the commands I have given you. And be sure of this: I am with you always, even to the end of the age.

Step Twelve is a three-part step. First, we have a Spiritual Awakening. I like to think of this as being ambushed by the Holy Spirit. We were once asleep in our sins, and now through the power of God, we have been awakened. In the Timothy passage above, Paul is telling Timothy how the love of God overcame him and awakened him to the love of Christ. This awakening made him a new person.

Through the power of the Holy Spirit and His work in our lives, we become alive. While the world around us does not change, our reaction to the world does change. There are still frustrating events, people and the like. We usually have the same quirks and fears. But we handle all matters differently. We are more at peace with ourselves, others and God. We go from feeling helpless, fearful and powerless - to a sense of great peace. Yes, at times, we will still have our fears and feelings of hopelessness, but now we have the Holy Spirit in us, guiding us along the path of life. These steps are a part of keeping us on track on that path, to stay focused on God. We have changed directions, from being self-centered to being Christ-centered.

The second part of Step Twelve is to carry this message to others, which is exactly what Jesus is saying in the Great Commission. The message is our Spiritual Awakening. The operative word here is, Go!? Out of our gratitude to Christ for his love for and mercy to us, we should want to help others. We should want to give them the good news. We are not to ignore others that are struggling in life as we are. We are to share with them the good news of our Spiritual Awakening and the effects it is having on our lives. I hope my life attracts people to me. I would rather be one to attract others, than to promote my awakening. The greatest question someone can ask me is what is it about you that is different? I want what you have.

To carry the message to others is not something we do to say we are better than others, or that we have all the answers to life and are going to show them how to live. In fact, we gain from being around others that are going through what we have been through in life. Going out benefits us as much as those to whom we take the message.

Third, we are to practice the principles that we have learned in these twelve steps, in all our affairs. We will not stay well if we do not stay on this wellness program. We cannot appropriate the grace of God to just one area of our life and hope the other areas stay intact. The life lessons that we are learning and practicing should permeate all areas of our lives, our homes, work and play. A natural habit of living rightly should flow from us.

So, that's it - Twelve Steps for Christian Living. Simple, no! Practical, yes! Can you do it? Of course you can. Is it easy? No way. Nowhere in the Bible do I find a passage, or even one verse, saying, "okay, now that you are a Christian, life is going to be a breeze." Life is hard. Life seems impossible to those without hope. Our hope is Christ. Our hope is the life after this life. Our hope is doing life right here on Earth. Our hope is in the knowledge of, and faith in, Christ.

My hope and prayer is that this survey of the Twelve Steps has been a blessing for you. Writing about and studying these steps has blessed me beyond what I thought was possible.

Chapter 9

Going Out

~~~

Part 1 – Personal Evangelism

"Neither do people light a lamp and put it under a bowl. Instead they put it on its stand, and it gives light to everyone in the house. ¹⁶ In the same way, let your light shine before men, that they may see your good deeds and praise your Father in heaven." Matthew 5:15 (NIV)

When I say the word "evangelist," what is the image that comes into your mind? A television preacher with really bad hair, begging for money? Or perhaps a stranger at your front door, interrupting your Sunday nap? You may have even read the title of this devotional and thought, "Oh brother, this one is not for me." I think when Jesus hears the word "evangelist," He sees you and me. He envisions all believers being light in a very dark world.

The problem for most of us is that we don't know where to begin when it comes to being a light for Christ in today's world. We are very comfortable being undercover Christians, just talking about God and Christ among our fellow Christians. We are scared to step outside the comfort zones of church and home, and to uncover our lamps. Let's look at some practical steps toward getting started on a path of being witnesses for Christ in all we do.

The first step on this path is taking an honest look at our own lives. The most compelling question you can ask yourself regarding your faith is, "If you were put on trial and the jury was your family, friends, coworkers, classmates, and other people in your sphere of influence, would your life provide enough evidence to convict you of being a Christian?" Are you living an authentic and consistent Christian life, no matter where you are or whom you're around? Are you the same person on the golf course as you are in Sunday school class? Do you treat your classmates, family members, fellow workers, the person in the restaurant, or the person at the checkout counter all the same? Can they tell that there is something different (in a positive way) about you? Can they tell your values are different than the world's values? A life of inconsistency severely diminishes your effectiveness as an example of Christ.

Secondly, once we get our own lives in order as much as humanly possible, then we earn the right to be heard by those people without Christ in our world. We need to build relationships with these people. Paul tells us to be in the world but not of the world. Be deliberate. I've learned to be very deliberate about building relationships with nonbelievers. Pray for God to put someone in your life, someone who needs you. He will honor that prayer.

You may be asking, "Now what, David? What in the world am I going to do if someone asks me about God?" Relax. Different people have different styles of evangelism. Peter was very confrontational, while Paul was very intellectual. Likewise, different personalities will respond to different styles of evangelism. All some people need is a simple question like, "Would you like to come to my church this weekend?" Or a simple, "We're having a great music program Wednesday night at my church. Would you like to join us?" Some of us find it very easy to say, "Life for me is better, now that I've discovered the Bible is applicable to my life." Find the style that best suits your personality and use it. The main thing is being the person that God wired you up to be.

In the next part of this chapter I will lay out some different styles of personal evangelism that are found in the Bible. As you finish the first part of this chapter, be in earnest prayer, asking for an honest assessment of your walk with Christ, as well as of your consistency. Would you be convicted of being a Christian, if you were tried by a jury of your peers?

Part 2 – Evangelism Approaches

In the first part of this chapter, I made two points: (1) we are all called to spread the Gospel and (2) we must first take a good look at our own walk with Christ before we can be effective witnesses for Him. This week I want to look at six different approaches to evangelism that are found in the Bible. My prayer is that you can get your hands around one of these approaches and use it to help spread the good news of Christ to people in your world. Jesus' plan was really simple: Share the Gospel with one person at a time, and see life after life changed by Him.

1. Testimonial Approach

"He replied, 'Whether he is a sinner or not, I don't know. One thing I do know. I was blind but now I see!'" John 9:25 (NIV)

This is one of my favorite verses in the Bible. Here we find a blind man who has been healed by Jesus. The Pharisees are interrogating the man and his family about Jesus. They do not believe that the man was once blind or that Jesus had miraculously healed him. The man's testimony was simply the truth. It was his story. It was not a theological debate, but a simple, "All I know is that I was once blind, but now I see!"

I think most of us have stories that are natural to tell. After all, we are telling people what happened to us. Sometimes all it takes when talking to a friend struggling with life is an encouraging testimony. You may say, "I know how empty, how lonely, how unfulfilled you feel. I once felt that way, but since I started journeying with Jesus, my life hasn't been the same. I was once blind but now I see."

2. Invitational Approach

"Then, leaving her water jar, the woman went back to the town and said to the people, 'Come, see a man who told me everything I ever did. Could this be the Christ?' They came out of the town and made their way toward him." John 4:28-30 (NIV)

In this passage, we find the Samaritan woman who had an encounter with Jesus by the well. After her experience, she ran back to town to invite the town's people to meet the Messiah. This approach to evangelism is one of the least threatening to most people. You simply invite them to your church. It may be a Sunday service, a mid-week Bible study, or a special event.

3. Service Approach

"In the city of Joppa there was a woman named Dorcas (Gazelle), a believer who was always doing kind things for others, especially for the poor." Acts 9:36 (LB)

God wires some people who love serving others. Dorcas was one of those people. Kind acts for other people, with nothing expected in return, seem to be less common these days. I love taking my kids to the homeless shelter and serving food. Invariably someone will ask, "Why do you do this?" We do it because we believe in doing what the Bible commands us to do. We serve out of gratitude for what Jesus has done for us. There are countless numbers of opportunities for service in your community. Let others see Christ working through you.

4. The Matthew Party Approach

"Soon Levi held a reception in his home with Jesus as the guest of honor. Many of Levi's fellow tax collectors and other guests were there." Luke 5:29 (LB)

After Matthew became a follower of Christ, he gave a party and invited all of his old friends and his new Christ-following friends to meet Jesus and each other. Matthew's approach is an interpersonal approach. It works well for those who enjoy spending a lot of time with people, developing mutual trust and deep relationships. Through this trust they are able to weave their faith into the lives of the people around them. My next-door neighbors had a "Matthew Party" during a snowstorm last year. They invited all the neighbors over for stew and hot chocolate. The husband said a wonderful prayer and the dinner conversation was low-key, but Christ found His way into the conversations often. I am sure that dinner has had an impact on some of our neighbors. Be creative and think of ways to have "Matthew parties" IF that is a style of evangelism that suits your personality.

5. Peter's Confrontational Approach

Then Peter stepped forward with the eleven apostles and shouted to the crowd, "Listen, all of you, visitors and residents of Jerusalem alike!" Acts 2:14 (LB)

While Peter is one of my favorites in the Bible, I am not sure if he is someone that I would pal around with on a regular basis. Peter was a very in-your-face kind of guy. God wired him that way, and used Peter's personality in Acts 2 to deliver a very confrontational sermon that resulted in over 3,000 people being saved. But this approach is a very specialized one. It should do only (1) if you have this gift from God and (2) if the person being confronted will respond to this style of evangelism. I have used this style only once in my life. It was with a very confrontational person and as God would have it, it succeeded with this particular person. Some people have the gift of this confrontational approach but unfortunately use it at the wrong times or on the wrong people. I cringe when I hear someone shouting to every passerby, Turn or burn!" I have had some people complain to me that they do not want anything to do with Christianity because the Christians they know are so obnoxious and annoying. If you do use Peter's approach, use it with care.

6. Intellectual Approach

"As was Paul's custom, he went there to preach, and for three Sabbaths in a row he opened the Scriptures to the people, explaining the prophecies about the sufferings of the Messiah and his coming back to life, and proving that Jesus is the Messiah. Some who listened were persuaded and became converts-including a large number of godly Greek men and also many important women of the city." Acts 17:2 (LB)

Obviously Paul was a gifted intellectual. God used his intellect to reach the "smart" people of Thessalonica. Some of my doctor friends are very natural in using this approach with their associates. Very calculated and logically-minded people need a very detailed explanation about who Jesus is. They most likely would not respond to the testimonial approach. Instead, their spiritual journey is paved with facts before they find real faith.

I hope you have stayed with me this far. Take a good look at your own life. Try to live out a consistent, authentic Christ like life. Find a style of evangelism that fits your personality. Pray for God to place people in your life who are without Christ. And most importantly, just be you. Be the person that God made you to be.

Part 3 – Caveats of Evangelism

"Therefore, if anyone is in Christ, he is a new creation; the old has gone, the new has come!" 2 Corinthians 5:16 (NIV)

I was reminded by correspondence from several friends and from personal experience of one of the greatest caveats about personal evangelism. I pray that this last section of the book will help you understand these traps that can discourage you from doing your part in advancing the cause of Christ.

A few years ago, a man in our church had the spiritual gift of evangelism. He was effective in door-to-door campaigns of witnessing. He never missed an opportunity to tell anyone willing to listen to the sensational news about Jesus Christ. He was bold and effective with some people, but not with everyone. I will never forget what he shared with me one day after a Bible study, in the parking lot of our church. With tears in his eyes and great frustration, he told me that his mother-in-law simply would not listen to the Gospel. She would not change. Over and over again, he kept saying, "I can't get her to change."

Some of you may express the same feelings regarding friends and family members. You are exhausted from trying to get people to change. Frustrated spouses go to church alone, while their mates sit at home waiting for them to return, so they can berate them or scoff at their church attendance. Family members, coworkers, acquaintances, and classmates sigh and walk away, when you try to share what Christ means to you. You walk away feeling defeated and deflated.

My friend in the parking lot gave up on church. I know of spouses and family members that give up on Christ. They are falling into a terrible trap that the great deceiver has laid out for them.

"The Spirit of the LORD will come upon you in power, and you will prophesy with them; and you will be changed into a different person." 1 Samuel 10:6 (NIV)

"As Saul turned to leave Samuel, God changed Saul's heart, and all these signs were fulfilled that day." 1 Samuel 10:9 (NIV)

Don't miss the point of the above verses. **You are not the change agent for a person's heart. Only through the Holy Spirit are hearts changed.** Please don't overestimate your own power, and for Heaven's sake, do not underestimate God's power. We are only the communication agent. God is the change agent. He is the catalyst. I read a recent study that said that on average, a person hears the Gospel seven times before responding to the message. Your time of sharing may be the first time, the fifth time, or sometimes even the seventh. Keep planting the seeds - tell the story, and above all else, let your life show it.